Chris Brace
May 1996.

BRITAIN AND REVOLUTIONARY FRANCE:
Conflict, subversion and propaganda

Edited by Colin Jones

Produced in conjunction with
the Western European Studies Centre,
University of Exeter

D1615536

EXETER STUDIES IN HISTORY No.5

Published by the University of Exeter 1983

EXETER STUDIES IN HISTORY

Editorial Committee

Prof I.A.Roots MA FSA FRHistS
M.Duffy MA DPhil
C.D.H.Jones BA DPhil
M.D.D.Newitt BA PhD FRHistS
B.J.Orme BA MPhil FSA

Publications

ISBN   0   85989   179   8

ISSN   0260   8626

Printed in Great Britain by A. Wheaton & Co. Ltd., Exeter

Contents

Acknowledgements

The Contributions in this volume by Michael Duffy, David Geggus, Marianne Elliott and Malcolm Cook were presented as papers to a conference on 'Britain and France in the 1790s' held at the University of Exeter on November 23rd-24th 1982. The conference was largely financed by the University of Exeter's Western European Studies Centre. Thanks are due to the latter's directors Stephen Mennell and Jeremy Noakes; to Juliet Curry and Noreen Welsh for their invaluable help with the typing and word-processing; and to Mike Rouillard for the cover design. Finally I should like to express my appreciation for the support and encouragement given by Michael Duffy and Malyn Newitt especially when, in the latter stages of production, sabbatical leave whisked me off from Exeter to Palavas-les-Flots!

The Editor

The Anglo-French Conflict 1789-1802

Events in France	The Anglo-French War	Events in Britain
	1789	
Outbreak of the French Revolution		
	1790	
		NOV. Burke's Reflections on the Revolution in France
	1791	
		APR. Pitt desists
AUG. Slave revolt in Saint Domingue	Secessionist overtures from French W.I. planters to British government	from ultimatum to Russia
	1792	
APR. War with Austria and Prussia		MAY. Proclamation against seditious writings
AUG. Overthrow of monarchy		
SEPT. Repulse of Prussian invasion	SEPT.-DEC. abortive secession of French	
NOV. Austrian Netherlands seized; Scheldt opened; Edict of Fraternity	Windward Islands in West Indies	NOV.-DEC. British warning to France on Scheldt decree and threat to Holland. Association Movement against 'Levellers and Republicans'
	1793	
JAN. Execution of Louis XVI	FEB 1. France declares war on Britain	FEB. Formation of the First Coalition against France
MAR. Vendée Revolt	MAR. France driven from Netherlands	
APR. Comité de Salut Public	FEB-JUNE. Agreements signed between French and British W.I. planters in London	
AUG. Levée en Masse		
	SEPT. Failure of British attack on Dunkirk; British occupy Toulon	
	NOV. British expedition sails for West Indies	
	DEC. British driven from Toulon	

1794

MAR–APR. British capture French Windward Islands

APR. Convention emancipates slaves

MAY. Pitt's Terror
MAY. Suspension of Habeas Corpus; arrest of leaders of radical societies

JUNE–DEC. Victor Hugues lands on Guadeloupe; drives out British, arms slaves

SUMMER/AUTUMN. Fall of Robespierre; end of Revolutionary Gov.

1795

JAN–FEB. French seize Holland

MAR. rebellions in British W.I.

Prussia, Holland, Spain make peace with France

MAY. Holland declares war on Britain

JUNE. British driven from St Lucia

JULY. British inspired emigre landing at Quiberon repulsed

JULY. Maroon War in Jamaica

JULY–SEPT. British take Ceylon and Cape of Good Hope

OCT. Food shortages; attack on king's coach

NOV. Inauguration of Directory

NOV. Abercromby expedition to W.I.

NOV. Treasonable practices and Seditious Meetings Act

1796

APR. Capture of Dutch S. American colonies of Demerara, Essequibo and Berbice

MAY. Bonaparte's conquest of Italy begins

MAY–JUNE. Abercromby recovers St Lucia and ends rebellions in Grenada and St Vincent
OCT.–DEC. abortive peace negotiations at Paris
DEC. '96–JAN. '97 gales thwart Hoche's invasion of Ireland

OCT. Spain declares war on Britain

1797

FEB. capture of Trinidad; defeat of Spanish fleet at St Vincent
MAR. Forcible disarming of Ulster

APR. Austria agrees to make peace with France; end of First Coalition

3

SEPT. Anti-royalist
coup of 18 Fructidor

JULY-SEPT. Abortive peace
negotiations at Lille

OCT. defeat of
Dutch fleet at
Camperdown; threat
of French invasion

1798

MAY. Bonaparte's
Egyptian expedition
AUG. Battle of the Nile;
Small French force lands
in Ireland; surrenders
(September)
MAY-OCT. British with-
draw from Saint Domigue

MAY-AUG. Irish
rebellion

1799

MAR. renewal of
continental war
JUNE. formation of
Second Coalition

Acts against
illegal
combinations; ban
on London Corresp-
onding Society and
United Englishmen;
Occupation of Dutch
Surinam

NOV. Bonaparte seizes
power
WINTER. Abortive rising
in Vendée

Russia withdraws from
war
JUNE. Austrians
defeated at Marengo

1800

Collapse of Second
Coalition

Food shortages and
discontent

Occupation of
Curacao in Dutch
West Indies

SEPT. Austrians defeated
at Hohenlinden

1801

JAN. Peace of Lunéville
with Austria

JAN. Full union
with Ireland comes
into effect; Pitt
resigns

MAR.-JUNE British drive
French from Egypt

APR. Armed Neutral-
ity of Baltic
Powers defeated at
Copenhagen;
Capture of Danish
and Swedish West
Indies

OCT. Preliminary terms
of peace signed in
London

1802

MAR. Peace of Amiens

French restore slavery
in Guadeloupe and
attempt to reconquer
Saint Domingue

Introduction

COLIN JONES

> We prided ourselves on our prejudices: we
> blustered and bragged with absurd vainglory; we
> dealt to our enemy the monstrous injustice of
> contempt and scorn; we fought him with all
> weapons, mean as well as heroic. There was no
> lie which we would not credit. I thought at one
> time of making a collection of the lies which the
> French had written against us and we had publish-
> ed against them during the war; it would be a
> strange memorial of popular falséhood. (1)

The present volume makes a contribution to what some historians
have dubbed the 'Second Hundred Years War' - the period between 1689 and
1815 for nearly half of which Britain and France were at war with one
another, and during which Anglo-French rivalry constituted a major axis
of European power politics. (2) Yet if in some senses the 1790s
represented the final episode in a secular struggle for European
supremacy, contemporaries were aware that the French Revolution transformed the nature and the intensity of the relationship of the two
societies. It is my aim, in the Introduction to the present volume, to
highlight some of the things that were novel and striking about the form
that the Anglo-French conflict took in this 'Revolutionary' decade.

For most of the eighteenth century, even when formally at war, the
French and the English had somehow contrived to be mutually admiring as
well as hostile and disdainful. Georgian England was forever indulging
in French fads and fancies, while 'Anglomania' was a recurrent leitmotiv
of the French Enlightenment. There were times, it is true, when Frenchmen might feel, as one determined Anglo-phobe put it, that 'before the
English learn that there is a God to be worshipped they learn that there
are Frenchmen to be detested'. The more ironical note struck by Oliver
Goldsmith was on balance, however, closer to the mark: he observed that,
"The English and the French seem to place themselves among the champion
states of Europe. Though parted by a narrow sea, yet they are entirely
of opposite characters; and from their vicinity are taught to fear and
admire each other."(3) That each nation had complementary characters was
a truism accepted in central and eastern Europe too. The scions of
Russian noble families who made the 'Grand Tour' of Western Europe, for
example, often remarked on the respective virtues of the two leading
nations of European politics: the French cultured, polished, fashion-
conscious, the English puritanical, industrious, commercially adept.(4)

5

This love-hate relationship between the English and the French in the eighteenth century was grounded in an intimate mutual knowledge. Once the harsh confessional strife of the wars of Louis XIV had been softened by the growing spirit of religious toleration, the two societies developed, even when at war with each other, an endless reciprocal flow of traders, travellers, artists, musicians, freemasons, farmers, scientists, students, engineers, industrialists, skilled workers, soldiers (the French government was only stopped officially from recruiting in Connaught and Munster in 1738, and the French king's Irish brigade had a more than ample native Irish contingent right down to its dissolution in 1791)(5) and, through all these channels developed an increasing interchange of ideas. This picture changed drastically after 1793. The clandestine export of skilled workers and of British technology was never totally stamped out during the Revolutionary and Napoleonic Wars, yet historians strongly underline the extent to which from the 1790s the relative technological isolation of the states of continental Europe from the burgeoning industrial economy of Britain considerably handicapped their economies. With Britain by 1800 within an ace of securing a virtual monopoly of overseas raw materials and markets, the British economy surged appreciably ahead of France, and made the latter's task of 'catching up' in the nineteenth century proportionately harder.(6)

There was also to be a new degree of ideological isolation between the two countries in the 1790s. Although they were never to be totally incommunicado - the postal services between them continued unabated, and the respective governments were among the most avid readers of each others newspapers - what had formerly been a flood of intellectual and cutural exchange was dwindling to little more than a trickle. English visitors to France now found themselves risking imprisonment as spies, and the appalling accents which had been the butt of French humour were now listened to with sullen suspicion. In England the government passed a panoply of measures for what Burke called 'war police': (7) the Traiterous Correspondence Act of 1793, for example, made treasonable offences many of the kinds of contact with France which private citizens had engaged in during every other war of the eighteenth century (trade, supply, money-lending, land purchase etc.).Such measures fanned the flames of what Robert Hole demonstrates below became a virulently xenophobic and reactionary campaign, and while the Revolutionaries in France brandished aloft the Rights of Man, political hacks and cartoonists in England cast doubt on whether the French even deserved to be regarded as fellow members of the human species. Wilful misrepresentation and ignorance thus came to replace the openness which had formerly conditioned the relationship between the two countries. There was certainly no ideological Maginot line across the Straits of Dover, but the distance from Paris to London seemed incomparably greater than before. The French author mentioned below by Malcolm Cook who claimed that his novel was published in Wimbledon was doubtless aware that, to most Frenchmen, this had suddenly become a location as exotic as Canton or Timbuktoo.

A major insulating medium keeping Britain and France apart in the 1790s was propaganda - and in particular government-inspired and even government-directed propaganda.Historians tend to see the Revolution as

marking a milestone in the history of propaganda. A term which originally meant the work of proselytisation conducted by the post-Tridentine
Catholic church was secularised and enlarged by the political and social
ideology which the Revolutionaries bade fair to disseminate throughout
Europe and even – as the activities of Victor Hugues, in the Caribbean,
for example, made clear – in the New World. Like charity, however,
propaganda began at home. As traditional forms of ensuring ideological
consensus broke under the impact of the Revolution, and as the growing
drift of anti-clericalism ruled out the time-hallowed use of the pulpit
as a means of government communication and persuasion, the way was open
for other ways of winning over the hearts and minds of the indigenous
population. The press, posters and official documents of every description were assiduously exploited as means of getting across political
messages.(8) From the time of the Directory onwards, even scrupulously
edited and decoratively embellished military bulletins from the front
served the same purpose (so flagrantly indeed, that under Napoleon the
phrase 'to lie like a bulletin' passed into popular usage).(9) These
motley forms of government propaganda were bolstered by a wide variety
of artistic and intellectual communication: poetry, theatre, popular
prints and engravings, and fictional writing all became vehicles for the
transmission of political ideas, and means of fostering a new sense of
social solidarity.

The content of all these different forms of propaganda and ideology
varied enormously. Yet it is worth remarking that the obverse of the
patriotic elan in France was a new blatant streak of Anglophobia, which
was grounded in the ignorance and distortion which now characterised
Anglo-French relations. Bonaparte's well-known evocation of 'perfidious
Albion' was merely the culmination of earlier waves of fury and hatred
aimed at France's oldest rival. From very early in the 1790s, in fact,
the Revolutionaries had heaped opprobrium on the head of prime minister
William Pitt, architect of the First Coalition, most steadfast opponent
of the Revolution among all European statesmen, paymaster of counter-
revolution and, it was widely held, active destabiliser of the French
economy. Recent research has demonstrated how relatively sparing and
discriminating the British government really was in the 1790s with its
money – certainly in comparison with the more luxuriant days of the
Fourth Coalition.(10) Yet in the eyes of Pitt's contemporaries and
opponents, 'Pitt's Gold' was ubiquitous and, for governments which
sometimes sought to obscure their own shortcomings and backslidings from
their citizens, it could cover a multitude of sins.

If propaganda was important in laying the foundations of French
expansion in Europe in the Revolutionary and Napoleonic period, it was
utilised with equal skill and success on this side of the Channel. As
Michael Duffy demonstrates below, an ideological commitment to counter-
revolution was one of the main planks of British foreign policy
throughout the 1790s. In purely diplomatic terms it was usually
subordinated, it is true, to the strategic considerations of maritime
and continental security, and it sometimes had to compete with long inbred traditions of isolationism. Yet, if nothing else, the Pitt
government's determination to meet the French Revolutionary propaganda
on its own terrain served a crucial legitimising political function
inside Britain. Doubtless events in the later 1790s (the naval mutinies

of 1797, the Irish rebellion of 1798) were serious enough to make
draconian repression understandable. Yet, as Marianne Elliott suggests
below, the expeditious winding up of many of the liberties of 'free-born
Englishmen' was initiated early in the 1790s, when the largely innocuous
links which the English and Irish democratic movements had forged with
the French were, in the harsh and distorting glare of government-
inspired propaganda, made to appear far more menacing and subversive
than they really were.

In Britain then, as in France, propaganda was as much for internal
consumption as for export – probably more so in Britain's case, in fact,
as the disillusionment of French counter-revolutionaries with their
English contacts suggests. Much credit for the artfulness and acumen
with which propaganda was utilised within Britain undoubtedly belonged
to prime minister William Pitt. Political manipulation at Westminster
went hand in hand with the active marketing of war among the nation at
large. The government actively sponsored propaganda tracts and the like
and, as in France, this elicited a strong grassroots response. The
constitutional sonorities of Burke and his acolytes filtered down
through society at large, by means of the variegated contributions of
Gillray, Hannah More and rabidly patriotic 'Church and King' mobs. So
saturated did the British public become with the propagandists' view of
the French, that it was with real surprise that visitors to France in
the 1790s and early 1800s encountered reality. The diplomats who composed the mission of Lord Malmesbury in 1796 to discuss peace terms with
the Directory, for example, were astonished to find how little the state
of France conformed with the image presented at home: society seemed
calm well-ordered and tranquil. One noted : "The exhausted state and the
degree of distress which I could discover in this country, I must
confess, fell short of the expectations which the various species of
plunder, exaction and cruelty which it was for several years submitted
to, had impressed upon my mind."(11) Similarly, in 1801, as the
negotiations at Amiens seemed to be about to signalise the resumption of
free and easy intercourse between the two societies (more than 20,000
Englishmen and women were supposed to have visited France before
hostilities resumed in 1803) (12) visitors were equally taken aback.
Expecting to find emaciated paupers and the ghastly traces of cannibals
and buveurs du sang, they found instead fat peasants and a seemingly
universal respect for good order.

This disparity between the official ideology and the prosperous
reality highlights the fact that British government propaganda served,
among other things, to justify a war record which was, in fact, far from
brilliant. From the vantage point of the early nineteenth century, the
balance sheet of the British war effort was not terribly impressive:
unparallelled interference in the internal affairs of her neighbours by
a country in which isolationist sentiments were always strong: continual
continental entanglements; a dubiously attritionist policy in the
Caribbean; consistent overestimation of the strength of the Revolution's
enemies in France; a series of ill-conceived and badly-managed expeditions (Quiberon Bay, the Helder etc.); a growing alienation of
potential allies in Europe; and, underlying it all, a persistent
tendency to overestimate Britain's resources and capabilities. Even
measures which laid the basis of Britain's eventual victory in the war

8

with France aroused little enthusiasm: the introduction of income tax in
1798, for example, was seen with jaundiced eye. Equally union with
Ireland in 1801 was considered by many as something of a poisoned
chalice. The comments of the Austrian foreign minister Thugut in 1795 in
summing up the British position might have stood as an epigraph for
their war effort over the whole decade: "It is true that England
disposes of immense means, but their effect is continually paralysed by
the absolute lack of well-organised direction; it consumes from the
start the most precious resources, but in the wastage of a prodigality
without real objective; everywhere it commits itself to huge costs,
everywhere it pays for the maintenance of troops, but without having any
effective combattants."(13)

Doubtless the limited successes which British forces carried off in
the Caribbean – and David Geggus reminds us below that the effects of
the West Indian committment were nowhere near as catastrophic as was
often made out at the time – and the more thoroughgoing domination of
the seas which the Royal Navy secured, helped assure the government of
support from commercial and manufacturing interests whose influence was
growing in these critical years of Britain's industrial transformation.
They certainly helped the government ride over the financial, economic
and social strains which were clearly apparent by the late 1790s.
Nevertheless the relatively slim return which the British government was
able to extract in the Peace of Amiens, for all the time money and
resources expended in the course of the previous decade, would, one
might have imagined, have set a question-mark against the wisdom of the
policies espoused by the Pitt government. Yet in fact, something akin to
the reverse was true: though Britain certainly had its Jacobins, the
political objectives of the government struck a generally warm and
responsive chord among the English people (hardly Irish), and the whole
decade witnessed a surge of popular loyalism, or demotic patriotism,
unmatched in the whole of the eighteenth century. Surely, if nothing
else, this was tribute to the effectiveness of government propaganda ?

Propaganda was thus a key element in ensuring state cohesion and
social solidarity on both sides of the Channel, and it fostered a degree
of active participation in warfare rarely if ever achieved before.
Service in the army or in the militia had been highly unpopular in
Ancien Regime France, and Alan Forrest has recently deflated some of the
rhetoric about la Nation armée and the levée en masse of the
Revolutionary wars by showing how this tradition continued into the
1790s: a large proportion of the male population went to surprisingly
great lengths (flight, fraud, precocious marriage, self-mutilation...)
in order to avoid joining up.(14) Nevertheless, if the rhetoric about
the Revolutionary armies was more than a little inflated at times, there
remained a substantial reality beneath the myths.(15) The French army,
in the Revolutionary decade, experienced a quantum leap in size – a
million and a half men were mobilised in 1793-4, about half of them
actually under arms, and the level of effectives remained at about
double the Ancien Regime levels down to the turn of the century. The Loi
Jourdan of 1798 which introduced conscription laid the basis of the
massive armies of Napoleonic Europe. In addition, the conduct of war was
transformed by the impact of the Revolution: the soldats-citoyens of the
Revolutionary forces would, in their patriotic commitment to the national

cause, perform in ways, and with an enthusiasm, quite unknown in Ancien Regime forces. Furthermore, French society and economy were far more closely integrated into the war effort than ever before - and never more so than at the height of the Terror in 1793-1794 when the Committee of Public Safety achieved a level of state regulation of the ecopnomy (state subsidies and nationalisations, price and wage controls, direction of labour etc.) unsurpassed in France or England until the twentieth century.

These developments in the impact of warfare on society at large were, in several classic respects, unparallelled on the other side of the Channel. Whereas in France, for example, the war contributed to a social paroxysm which saw the traditional ruling class either neutralised or liquidated, in Britain the experience of the 1790s brought ruling class and government into a particularly close alliance. In France, the army was utterly transformed; in Britain, the Ancien Regime mix of a patrician officer corps commanding a rank-and-file it chose to view as the 'scum of the earth' was still very much in existence on the field of Waterloo. Nor did Britain renounce the traditional orientation of its defence around the Royal Navy.

The maintenance of Britain's naval supremacy in the wars against France was only, however, achieved at a massive cost - which underlined the importance of the impact of war in Britain as well as in France. Armies - and in particular Revolutionary armies, which even from 1792 were reverting to an atavistic 'living-off-the-land' policy - were far cheaper than navies because the latter were capital- rather than labour-intensive. France had discovered this to her cost, and had only been able to build up its naval forces into anything like a match for Britain in 1793-4 by dint of the kind of intense economic regulation which was politically unviable after the fall of Robespierre.(16) If Britain ruled the seas during the Revolutionary and Napoleonic wars, this was primarily because she alone was willing and able to make the kind of financial commitment which this entailed. The £1500 millions which the wars cost Britain in loans and taxes were three or four times what they cost the French. And if the 315,000 British men whose lives were lost in those wars were less than the million Frenchmen who died in them, this nevertheless represented a pretty substantial loss in a population about half the size of France's. The ways in which warfare cut into British society in the 1790s may have been less patently dramatic than they were in France - the income tax comes rather lower on the histrionic register than the Reign of Terror, for example, and even buoyant British economic indices have little of the human and dramatic appeal of, say, the levée en masse. But the cuts were deep - and deeply felt. It was probably largely because of the massive expansion of its economy as the Industrial Revolution got underway that Britain was able to sail through the 1790s so relatively serenely. And it was to be her experience of that Industrial Revolution, along with the political Revolution taking place on the other side of the Channel and the mudslinging which both Britain and France had engaged in during the 1790s, which was to put Anglo-French relations in the century ahead on an entirely new footing.

Notes

1. W.M Thackeray, The Four Georges, London, 1867, p.153.

2. See the section, 'The Second Hundred Years War' by J.Meyer and J.Bromley in D.Johnson, F.Bedaride, F.Crouzet (eds), Britain and France. Ten Centuries, London, 1980.

3. Both these quotations are taken from D.Jarrett, The Begetters of Revolution: England's involvement with France 1759-89, London, 1973, p.40, p.18.

4. I would like to thank Dr Janet Hartley of the School of Eastern European and Slavonic Studies, London, for information on this point.

5. J.Bromley, 'Britain and Europe in the 18th Century', History, 1981, p.397.

6. Cf. for example, the relevant sections of D.Landes, The Unbound Prometheus, Cambridge, 1969; and R.Davis, The Rise of the Atlantic Economies, London, 1973 for discussion of these points.

7. Cited in C.Emsley, in his British Society and the French Wars 1793-1815, London, 1979, p.21.

8. See Alison Patrick's interesting article, 'Paper, Posters and People: Official Communication in France, 1789-1794', Historical Studies, 1978.

9. G.Best, War and Society in Revolutionary Europe 1770-1870, London, 1982, p.119.

10. Especially J.M.Sherwig, Guineas and Gunpowder: British Foreign Aid in the Wars with France,1793-1815, Cambridge Mass, 1969.

11. The Duke of Buckingham and Chandos (ed), Memoirs of the Court and Cabinets of George the Third, London, 1853, vol 2 p.356.

12. J.Deschamps, Entre la Guerre et la Paix: les Iles brittaniques et la Révolution française,1789-1803, Brussels, 1949, p.149.

13. Cited in M.Duffy, 'British War Policy: the Austrian Alliance, Oxford D.Phil thesis, 1971, p.220.

14. See A.Forrest, The French Revolution and the Poor, Oxford, 1981, esp. chapter 8.

15. C.Jones, 'The Welfare of the French Footsoldier', History, 1980, for an introduction to this topic.

16. Cf. N.Hampson, La Manie de l'An II: Mobilisation de la Flotte de l' Océan, 1793-4, Paris, 1959; and G.Best, op. cit., 85ff.

British Policy in the War against Revolutionary France

MICHAEL DUFFY

Although the British government was the last of the major European powers to declare its hostility to Revolutionary France, Britain was to prove the most persistent opponent of France throughout the Revolutionary and Napoleonic period. Once war was declared in 1793 there were to be little more than two years of peace before 1815. Throughout the long struggle, the basic British aims remained more or less those enunciated at the beginning by the Pitt ministry. The final peace settlement of 1814-5 in many of its details as well as in its broad essentials was that developed by Pitt and his colleagues between 1793 and 1801 while they supervised the war against Revolutionary France. (1) The objectives and the prolonged fight to achieve them are best explained through four main themes which determined the conduct of Pitt and his successors: namely, maritime security, continental security, isolationism and counter-revolution. In order to illuminate the bases of British policy in the 1790s, each of these themes will be linked, in what follows, to a key date close to the minds of Pitt and his colleagues - though in fact these dates represent only the most recent imperatives in policies long inbred into British prejudices.

1. Principles of British policy towards France.

The first theme is that of maritime security, and the immediate starting date for its consideration is 5 September 1781. On that day a French fleet barring the mouth of Chesapeake Bay drove off a British fleet which was attempting to relieve Lord Cornwallis' army, trapped by a Franco-American army at Yorktown, Virginia. Cut off from help, Cornwallis surrendered a month later and Britain abandoned its attempt to recover its rebel American colonies. French seapower had demonstrated its ability to disrupt the British empire, which was generally regarded as one of the main foundations of British maritime security. In the same war, between 1778 and 1783, the French navy seized much of Britain's rich West Indian empire and in 1779 a combined Franco-Spanish fleet had sailed unmolested up and down the Channel.

These harrowing reminders of the precarious nature of British
maritime security were not to be forgotten over the next thirty years.
After 1783, Pitt's government embarked on an extensive programme of
naval rearmament, and when war broke out again in 1793, Henry Dundas,
Pitt's war minister, looked to the destruction of France's navy and of
its overseas empire on which French sea-power was founded, as Britain's
main aim. Writing in July 1793 of his plans to seize France's
possessions in the West and East Indies, Dundas explained that 'success
in those quarters I consider of infinite moment, both in the view of
humbling the power of France, and with the view of enlarging our
national wealth and security'. (2) Dundas intended to destroy the
French empire in the same way that France had nearly destroyed that of
Britain between 1778 and 1783, which Dundas, who had been a member of
Lord North's government on that former occasion, remembered only too
well. The conquest of the French empire would produce a major reduction
in French trade and trained seamen and a corresponding increase in those
of Britain, and thus put Britain beyond serious danger in future from
the French navy, so ensuring British maritime security.

The second, related theme is that of continental security, and the
key date for Pitt's government in this case was 27 October 1787. On
that day, France signed a convention with Britain in Paris officially
renouncing any intention of interfering in the internal affairs of
Holland, and Pitt thereby achieved a great victory in winning Holland
back from French domination. The victory was cemented in the following
year by the establishment of a Triple Alliance between Britain, Holland
and Prussia which ended the international isolation in which Britain had
plunged to defeat in the American War. It was a major step towards
rebuilding maritime security in that the Dutch navy was transferred to
the British side in the Anglo-French contest for sea power, and Dutch
ports facing the mouth of the Thames no longer threatened invasion or
attacks on British trade. It was a substantial step towards commercial
security too in that ascendancy over Holland guaranteed entry of British
goods into Europe in wartime through a country that already provided
Britain with its second-biggest European trade balance in peace time,
and which was situated between France and Germany, with which area
Britain maintained an even more favourable trade balance. Although
Prussia was allowed to slip away from the Triple Alliance in 1791, the
British government clung to its newly restored Dutch connection as the
bulwark of British maritime, commercial and political interests in
north-west Europe. The maintenance of Holland as a client state of
Britain was an object particularly dear to Pitt whose greatest foreign
policy success it marked, and also to the Foreign Secretary Lord
Grenville who, in a junior position, had played a leading part in that
success, having been sent as Pitt's 'eyes' on special missions to both
Holland and France in 1786-7.

It was the renewed threat to the British hold on Holland that drew
the ministers at last into the open against France in November 1792. To
recover that hold became one of their major objectives when Holland fell
to the French in early 1795. As the war developed and the French
Revolution expanded beyond France's southern and eastern frontiers too,
so Britain came to have a wider view of continental security in seeking
to return France within its former frontiers and even to diminish these.

13

Throughout, however, the most sensitive area of the Continent for
British interests, as it had been for centuries, was this area
immediately opposite it across the Channel: Holland and, in order to
protect both Holland and Britain, the Austrian Netherlands (modern
Belgium) - the provinces between Holland and France. Even the
imperially-minded Dundas admitted in July 1793 that 'the most prominent
object of the war' was the safety of Holland:

> We are bound not only by the faith of treaty but by our
> immediate interests as a Nation to secure the
> independence of Holland, [he claimed, adding that] it
> has been assumed (justly in my opinion) as a corollary
> from this, that we must, if possible, retain the
> Netherlands in the House of Austria, as the only secure
> barrier to the United Provinces against the power and
> ambition of France. (3)

A strong power with a considerable army was necessary in Belgium to stop
France expanding its power and influence, domino-fashion, up the north-
western seaboard of Europe, excluding British political and commercial
influence, and creating a potent threat to British trade and to the
British coasts.

Thus far it can be seen that British interest in the French
Revolution was traditional and was directed towards its centuries-old
fear of France and French influence rather than against the Revolution
per se. This attitude was reinforced by a third theme, which might seem
strange in the light of the struggle which followed, and that was
isolationism. The strength of isolationist sentiment among the British
public was brought sharply home to Pitt's government in the midst of its
crisis with Russia in early 1791. Acting in cooperation with Prussia,
ministers sent Russia an ultimatum demanding its withdrawal from the
fortress of Ochakov, which the Russians had seized from Turkey and which
was believed to command the navigation of the Dniester, a strategic
point British ministers wanted kept open for commerce. However, the
political nation was unwilling to fight for such a remote object, and
withdrew its support, so that on 16 April 1791 the Cabinet was obliged
to recall its ultimatum and climb down. The shock of this sudden
withdrawal of public confidence made Pitt extremely wary of public
opinion for ever after - and wary also of too great an involvement in
Continental politics. As an Under-Secretary at the Foreign Office wrote
in March 1792,

> I conceive that after the rub we have lately had, any
> new interference in foreign politics further than what
> may be absolutely necessary for the immediate
> preservation of our Alliance [with Holland], is a matter
> hardly to be looked for. (4)

When in the spring of 1792 war broke out between France and the German
powers Austria and Prussia, the British government declared its
neutrality. When the course of the Revolution, and in particular the
French repulse of a Prussian invasion in September, stimulated a growing
demand for constitutional reform from British radicals at all levels,
ministers chose to deal with the crisis as a domestic issue unrelated to
the French Revolution and to be solved by isolation from Europe,
increased wages, lower taxes, and campaigns at home in suppport of the
constitution and against the spread of sedition. (5)

BRF-B

The one thing that could drive ministers out of this isolationist shell, as indicated above, was a threat to their Dutch alliance. This emerged in November 1792 when the French overran the Austrian Netherlands and declared the River Scheldt open to navigation in defiance of the treaty rights of Holland, through whose territory the Scheldt had its outlet into the North Sea. News of the French declaration was received in London on 26 November. It seemed to indicate a deliberate French attempt to overawe the Dutch, and ministers were prepared to fight to prevent this, for the reasons already indicated. It was not, however, a decision lightly taken, for it put at hazard the great increase in trade and industry which Pitt had seen as a product of peace. The Prime Minister protested to Dundas that 'it is indeed mortifying to be exposed to so many interruptions of a career the most promising that was ever offered to any country'. (6) Having taken the decision, however, ministers stuck to it when it became apparent that the French, truculent with victory, would not climb down. Thereafter they manoeuvred in a war of words to make the French appear in the wrong in the eyes of British public opinion and to provoke the French into making the actual declaration of war and so appearing the aggressor. In this at least they succeeded, for on 1 February 1793 France declared war on Britain.

Even the French declaration of war, however, did not destroy the inherently isolationist impulse of the British public. The radicals and the followers of Charles James Fox among the Parliamentary opposition protested loudly against the war, while many more Britons remained suspicious of expensive continental wars and entangling alliances with untrustworthy and despotic European monarchs. Such prejudices were a perpetual restraint on British war policy.

The final theme which acted as a determinant of British policy is that of counter-revolution. The Revolution first affected Anglo-French relations in the negotiations between November 1792 and the outbreak of war in February 1793. At this stage it affected the means rather than the ends of British policy. Throughout the pre-war crisis British concern was to remove the threat to its Dutch ally by securing French revocation of the Scheldt decree and by looking to an eventual French evacuation of the Austrian Netherlands. At this stage, ministers were not concerned to overthrow the Revolution. So long as the French government agreed to confine itself within its own frontiers, and in particular to renounce the famous decree of 19 November 1792 in which the French National Convention had declared its fraternity with all peoples who sought liberty, then British ministers would have been satisfied. Unfortunately the means which they adopted to secure these ends were to present as tough and as uncompromising a front as was possible, lest any gesture of conciliation be interpreted as a sign of weakness which would encourage the French in their pretensions and also lead them to promote subversion in Britain. Since the French government took much the same kind of stance, there was never much chance of a settlement.

From the French declaration of war on 1 February 1793 - our final policy-making date - the fact of the French Revolution came to influence the ends as well as the means of British policy. Till then ministers were ready to regard the Revolution as a purely internal matter, provided the French kept it as such. Grenville fended off suggestions from the German powers and Russia that Britain should intervene to restore the French monarchy. The furthest he would go was to press for the safety of Queen Marie-Antoinette and the removal of the decrees against the émigrés. The outbreak of war, however, changed all this. It showed that there was no conciliation or sense of responsibility in the revolutionary government - that the Revolution had become an international problem and if possible should therefore be eradicated. Even now the ministers' stated reasons for this change of attitude were coolly practical rather than missionary or idealistic: they wanted a guarantee that when peace was restored it would be kept. The instability of the Revolution, in which government succeeded government, and the whole course of affairs seemed at times to depend on the whim of the Paris mob, could give no security for this. Only a government founded on a monarch's sense of personal responsibility and secure in the broad support of the French people could, it was thought, provide such a guarantee.

This latter conclusion - the need for the broad support of the French people - dictated the form of monarchical settlement that ministers wished to impose on the French. While urging the French people to support the monarchy in Declarations in late 1793, Pitt and Grenville had no wish to stipulate the precise form of monarchical government that the French should receive: such an issue was too contentious to secure the general rallying together of internal opponents of the Revolution in France which they sought.

At the same time ministers had clear ideas of what they did not want. They did not want the entire reestablishment of arbitrary monarchy, which Grenville thought 'neither practicable nor desirable'. Nor did Grenville wish the restoration of the old judicial system of parlements, which had constantly caused political upheaval in the old régime, or the renewal 'of those odious personal exemptions which all the cahiers of the deputies of the First Assembly concurred in wishing to abolish and also of those feudal rights, the oppression of which was, in many provinces, the principal cause of arming the peasants against the proprietors of the land'. On the other hand, Grenville thought a return to the Constitution of 1791 equally undesirable - that had swung too far to the side of democracy and produced a system of government nullity which led to further revolution. Equally the confiscations of crown, church and émigré property could not be sanctioned, though Grenville recognised that some means would have to be found of conciliating the purchasers of that property and also the holders of assignats which were issued on the security of such property. Generally ministers hoped that the French could find for themselves some middle way between absolutism and the Constitution of 1791. It should be achieved, it was thought, not by reassembling the Estates General - Grenville thought that this would involve too many dissensions over precedent - but rather by some entirely new constitution-making body, an Assembly of Notables or some Convention expressly differing from all past legislative bodies. The new system of government which this would establish would incorporate both a monarch and a 'deliberating Assembly', and it should be backed by a religious restoration.

Grenville argued that 'whatever party really wishes to restore public peace in France must see that the bulk of the people there can never be brought back to the habits of industry and subordination but by the aid of religion'. He wanted 'some decent maintenance' confirmed for ministers of the established religion, and he wanted 'men of rank and liberal education' to be encouraged to engage in that profession by the prospect of more considerable rewards - he believed that the low state of the French clergy before the Revolution had removed a powerful barrier to that upheaval. All changes from the Ancien Régime should, however, be determined in a period of tranquillity and order after the Jacobin Revolution had been destroyed. In the meantime, ministers proposed to wipe the slate clean by restoring as far as possible the administration and officials of 1789 in areas of France which they conquered unconditionally. (7)

2. The attempt to implement British policies.

In the event, three of the themes on which Britain fought the war - maritime security, continental security and counter-revolution - were brought to a successful culmination in 1814-5, albeit at the price of sacrificing the fourth - isolation - until successive governments shook themselves free of continental entanglements again in the 1820s. Why did it take so long to achieve these ends? Two points can quickly be made by way of explanation. One is the sheer vigour generated by the Revolution in France. The regeneration of its administrative institutions and the throwing up of energetic and able leaders through careers being opened up to talent mobilised all the latent power in an advanced nation whose population was not much less than 30 millions. Second, Britain, with a population of only 13 to 15 millions, was trying to achieve something it had never contemplated before, namely, the total defeat of France and the overthrow of its government. The magnitude of these aims was unprecedented in the previous century of endemic Anglo-French conflict. Each of the four themes of British foreign policy in this period, moreover, contained elements which hindered the achievement of the others and thereby made the task even more difficult.

a) maritime security.

The bid to achieve maritime security was the policy aim over which the British government had most control since it was to be achieved largely from Britain's own resources. It was a matter in which, although great success was achieved, ministers could never be quite sure that they had clinched their victory while France had the capacity to renovate its resources from neighbouring maritime powers on the continent. The main focus of the Anglo-French contest for overseas empire was in the West Indies. It is examined by Dr Geggus below. Suffice it to say here that the British offensive in 1793-4 achieved great success, which was then jeopardised by a French-inspired slave revolt in which, perhaps fortuitously, the French proved the long-term losers. In Europe, ministers planned to attack and destroy the French naval bases but failed. They were repulsed from Dunkirk in 1793; Toulon was surrendered to them by the royalists on conditions which did not allow the destruction of the arsenal and before they had sufficient

manpower to secure it, so that it was lost at the end of 1793 with only
partial damage inflicted on the French warships and stores during a
hasty evacuation; while attempts projected on Brest for 1794 and 1800
failed to materialise through lack of troops and through the inability
of the royalists of western France to sustain a major diversion.
Ultimately it was left to the navy to achieve what it could by bringing
French squadrons to battle – but this constituted only a bit-by-bit
attrition of French seapower rather than an immediate and major
crippling of its resources, and it left time for the French to exploit
their superiority on land to seize the resources of their continental
neighbours and, hydra-like, to be continually producing new resources to
replace those lost in battle. Britain was thus led into employing
similar methods against those neighbours, so as to destroy their
maritime resources as well as those of the French. Between 1795 and
1800, it captured almost all the Dutch colonies and in 1799 it seized
the Dutch naval base at the Helder and carried off the Dutch fleet. Its
efforts against the larger and more populous Spanish empire were less
successful (except for the capture of Trinidad in 1796), and attacks on
the Spanish naval bases of Ferrol and Cadiz failed in 1800.

In the final analysis, therefore, Britain did not possess
sufficient resources of its own to achieve the total destruction of
French seapower which it sought. It did not possess sufficient
resources successfully to pursue its objectives of maritime and
continental security simultaneously, far less to restore monarchy to
France as well. Even in pursuit of maritime security alone, Britain
lacked resources to attack French naval bases in Europe at the same time
as the French empire. Dundas said in 1793 that if he were called upon
to choose between continental and maritime objectives, he should find
the choice a very disagreeable one. He hoped, however, not to have to
make such a choice because he believed that Britain possessed resources
enough for both. (9) He was proved wrong, and the need to make choices
produced many Cabinet and public wrangles over priorities in the years
that followed.

Britain had enough ships but insufficient soldiers to accomplish
its maritime objectives, but it found that when it tried to supplement
its own resources by looking to help from continental powers, it was
frequently thwarted by the effect of this very effort to secure maritime
and commercial supremacy (the two being inextricably intertwined). Not
only did its efforts to throttle French trade lead to clashes with
neutral shipping powers (it led to near war with the United States of
America in 1794, and to war with the Armed Neutrality of the Baltic
States in 1801), but it found that few foreign governments were willing
actually to help it achieve a maritime monopoly. Reports from British
diplomats abroad abound with echoes of Lord Minto's warning from Vienna
in 1800 of 'the universal jealousy, envy and indisposition which pervade
Europe, I believe, towards the supposed monopoly of trade and specie
enjoyed by England. We are represented as making war, and inciting all
other nations to join us, merely for its profits'. Because of the
superiority of its trade and maritime power, wrote Lord Carysfort from
Berlin, 'Great Britain [was] evidently giving more alarm and jealousy to
Europe than France'. When ministers appealed to other powers for troops
to help secure Toulon in 1793, they received a very lukewarm response.

Indeed the closer the British got to securing their maritime objectives,
the further away they got from securing their continental objectives,
since the other European powers looked to maintaining France as the only
possible balance to Britain on the oceans. Admittedly the continental
complaints about British egotism, profiteering and monopoly came loudest
when those powers were on the defensive against France and saw little
chance of securing any advantage themselves, but it is interesting to
see, as late as 1813-4, the sensitivity of the European powers on these
matters and also British realisation of the need to conciliate them. (10)

b) continental security.

The British effort to achieve maritime security therefore was a
major obstacle to its bid to achieve continental security but there were
many others too. Britain clearly could not take on the French army on
its own in Europe. It needed a 'continental sword' and ideally it
looked to uniting all the powers of Europe against France in a grand
coalition similar to the Grand Alliance which had defeated Louis XIV at
the beginning of the century. Dundas told the Commons in February 1793
that ministers wished to 'bring down every power on earth to assist them
against France'. (11) Significantly, such a universal European
combination was not achieved until 1813-4. A considerable obstacle here
of course was the differing interests of the various courts of Europe.
The days were long past when France was generally accepted as the major
danger to everyone. Now Prussia and Austria competed for dominance in
central Europe and both were suspicious in turn of Russian
expansion from the east. Spain, as a maritime power with a large
overseas empire, was particularly sensitive to British overseas
aggrandisement. The problem for any British government was how to
reconcile these conflicting interests and turn everyone against France.
Ministers soon discovered that there was no easy way of doing this.
Grenville constructed the First Coalition of 1793 around a minimum
objective - the restoration of all French conquests - despite the fact
that the British government wanted much more than this, because he
discovered that there was no chance of quick agreement on achieving
more. He had to try to build for a more positive outcome out of private
deals with individual powers thereafter.

Basically, there were three things that British ministers could try
to do so as to glue together a positive European alliance to secure the
continental objectives they had in mind. First, they could seek to
convince the other powers that France was their greatest danger. Though
they never ceased repeating this argument, however, its potency was
reduced by European fear of British aggrandisement and by the concern of
other powers for local and more immediate interests. Second, they could
buy support in Europe by means of loans and subsidies. The Pitt
ministry and its immediate successors were, however, reluctant to do
this on a scale which would outweigh all other considerations. Partly
this was because until Pitt built up a stronger tax capacity with the
introduction of income tax in 1798-9, and until British commerce
expanded to exploit the monopoly being slowly won, then there was simply
not enough money to go round. Equally, there was strong isolationist
feeling against Britain becoming, in Grenville's words, the 'milch cow'
of Europe. Public opinion had no wish to see other powers escape what

were regarded as their responsibilities and for the entire financial burden to be thrown onto Britain. Grenville in particular took the line that unless those powers felt they had a more pressing interest at stake that was worth fighting for, then Britain would get very little return for its money. Consequently during the war against Revolutionary France between 1797 and 1802, Britain paid out only nine and a half million pounds sterling in subsidies and six and a quarter millions in loans. In the subsequent Napoleonic Wars, financial assistance was to be stepped up drastically to forty nine and a half millions in subsidies and six hundred thousand pounds in loans, but even then over half of that sum (twenty six and a quarter millions in all) was only paid out in the last three years between 1813 and 1815 when Britain finally swamped Europe with financial glue in an all-out effort to defeat Napoleon. 'Pitt's gold' was thus a much scarcer commodity than the French Revolutionaries liked to think. (12)

As a consequence of this, British ministers looked to a third method of glueing alliances together, that of offering territorial incentives. Not surprisingly, this was fraught with problems. First, there was the problem of matching these incentives to Britain's particular desire for the security of Holland and the Netherlands. Initially, a straightforward solution here appeared to be to secure Austrian support against France by backing the expansion of the Austrian Netherlands at French expense, so as to provide a much stronger buffer for Holland against France. This became the cornerstone of British diplomacy for the first four years of the war. It created the problem, however, of binding Austria's rival, Prussia, to fight for Austrian aggrandisement - a problem which was never resolved. Nor was this sufficiently powerful an inducement to maintain an Anglo-Austrian alliance: isolationist prejudice in Britain prevented the government from giving a firm pledge to continue fighting until specific frontier areas were acquired for the Austrian Netherlands, while the Austrians themselves had other interests in Poland, in Italy and in Germany which they increasingly looked to when the war was going badly. Thereafter, Britain looked for new solutions to the Netherlands problem which only served to alienate Austria, which remained the European power most disposed to fight France. Austrian fears that Britain would dispose of the Netherlands without consulting Vienna wrecked the promising 1799 campaign against France.

A second problem about territorial incentives was the British insistence that these should be at France's expense and not at that of lame ducks like Poland. Isolationist prejudice amongst the British public led ministers to deplore and to try to ignore the Partitions of Poland in the 1790s despite the undoubted fact that these Partitions distracted the three major military powers of Europe (Austria, Prussia, Russia) from the war against France. By trying to pretend that the Polish problem did not exist, and demanding that everyone should concentrate on the French issue, ministers willingly blinded themselves to the extent of the distraction that Poland created. Even in 1795, when it was glaringly apparent that the quarrel over the final Partition was holding up the campaign against an exhausted France, ministers resolutely refused money to their allies Russia and Austria to get the Polish business over with by forcing Prussia to climb down. Ministers wanted to keep Prussia in the war and not alienate it, and they were acutely aware of - indeed they shared in - the popular dislike of the rape of Poland. As in the Ochakov crisis of 1791, the British government was not going to commit itself in a remote and unpopular cause, and to do so might in turn jeopardise popular support for the French war.

The third problem about territorial incentives was that if they were to be at France's expense, this would hardly help British hopes of restoring monarchy in France. As Grenville began making his territorial deals in 1793 it soon became apparent that if they all came off, the consequence would be a France reduced to its frontiers before the expansion of Louis XIV: Austria was looking to secure Flanders and Alsace-Lorraine, Piedmont-Sardinia wanted part of Provence, Britain was trying to persuade Spain to take territory in south-western France rather than in the French empire, while Britain intended to take the French empire itself. In their endeavours to secure counter-revolution in France, ministers hid the extent of these aims from the French. They admitted that Britain would look for an indemnity, but only said that this would be outside Europe - and they said nothing about the claims of their allies. This sort of approach was grounds for only temporary success, for no restored monarchy could survive the humiliation of such enormous cessions. Founded in humiliation, it would fall swiftly. Presumably this must eventually have occurred to Pitt and his colleagues, for when French expansion gave them another way out they took it: by 1798, they were prepared to see France retain its pre-war European boundaries and for Britain's allies to recoup themselves from French conquests in Europe. In contrast to their attitude to Poland, British ministers took the ruthless line that any small state or province unable to defend itself against the French lost its automatic right to restoration and came under consideration for amalgamation with another state which was better able to resist. In this way all the small states of Italy and on the west bank of the Rhine came up for grabs. Ministers planned to amalgamate Holland and the Netherlands, and they announced their own intention of retaining parts of the Dutch and Spanish maritime empires at the peace. Continental security would come less from reducing France's size in Europe than from increasing the size of the other large and medium powers at the expense of the smaller ones, and from a new system of collective security by which the major powers pledged to come to each others' assistance by guaranteeing each others' territory against French attack. This plan, worked out in the course of 1798, became the eventual basis of the peace settlement of 1814-5. It took six years of war, therefore, for Britain to work out a basis of continental security flexible enough to take account of most of the interests of the other powers, though it took more than a decade longer than that for them all to accept that they might get a better deal within this British system than by trying on their own outside it.

   c) isolationism.

It has been seen above how isolationism imposed limitations on the British government's freedom of action in its diplomacy. Isolationism meant that every diplomatic move had to be proved useful to the French war to which the bulk of the nation was committed. It meant that

ministers could never make firm commitments to continue the war
indefinitely until specific objectives were attained: they could never
be sure of public support lasting, and were afraid that any such
unlimited pledge would alienate the public all the quicker. The lesson
of Ochakov in 1791 had been that public support might be withdrawn at
any moment, and ministers worked hard to keep the public in line,
particularly when part of Pitt's own following, led by Wilberforce,
began to question the desirability of continuing the war in 1795.
Thereafter Pitt felt that, if he was to persuade the nation to continue
or increase its exertions, he had to show that he was willing to make
peace on reasonable terms, and that it was France that was being
unreasonable. Hence the peace proposals of 1795 and 1796, which played
their part in panicking Britain's allies into looking after their own
interests: they were afraid that Britain was about to leave them in the
lurch as it had done in 1711 and in 1762. Isolationism thus impeded
government efforts to form lasting alliances to bring the war to a
successful conclusion. Yet isolationism was also, paradoxically, one of
the main features keeping Britain at war with France until the final
victory. The public believed that Britain could isolate itself from the
disasters on the continent and, by reorientating their economy to the
trade monopoly overseas, that they could find the resources to continue
to fight France whatever happened in Europe. Above all their contempt
for the European despots meant that their morale was never totally
shattered by continental defeats. The French Foreign Office agent,
Otto, reported almost in despair from London in 1801:

> Would you attack Britain through its allies? It affects
> not to know them at the moment when they cease to be
> useful. Even Hanover is regarded as foreign to its
> interests: you could have burnt Vienna without giving a
> single care to the public in London. When I have said
> that the Russians have been sacrificed in Holland and
> Switzerland they reply that they were paid for it. (13)

Such an attitude hardly endeared Britain to potential allies but it
accounts for much of the national resilience in the face of the immense
catastrophes that the British public watched as coalition after
coalition which their governments constructed fell apart in mutual
recriminations and were destroyed by French power.

d) counter-revolution.

The spirit of counter-revolution may also have inspired the British
public to keep going, but in the nation which has been hailed as the
bastion of counter-revolution in the Revolutionary-Napoleonic period
this was probably the least powerful of the major British considerations
here discussed. Few people were prepared to fight to the death to
restore monarchy in France. Right from the start, Pitt hedged his bets
on this matter by stating that while a restoration was the most
desirable solution he would not rule out a settlement with any
government that showed a spirit of moderation and which seemed able to
last and to enforce a peace. (14) Subsequent peace negotiations with
the Directory and with Napoleon confirmed this attitude. The counter-
revolutionary stiffening to British policy came from a few influential
individuals rather than from a unanimous national mood. Burke and
Windham were the most vociferous, Grenville the most influential. While

the Foreign Secretary was prepared to go some way in Pitt's policy for the sake of government unity, he came more and more to believe that in the long course of history this was indeed a war to the death. He thought the outcome in the long term was doubtful. He wrote in 1797 that

> an entire and radical cure is hopeless. The evil was deeply rooted in the political state of the different nations of Europe, and it has acquired by the success of France a degree of strength and vigour which not even a complete counter-revolution there would counterbalance. It must I fear be expected that the greatest part of the next century will be as much distracted by wars of constitution and government and by struggles between Monarchy, Aristocracy and Democracy as former centuries have been by Wars of Religion or territorial aggrandisement. (15)

To Grenville, however, this was not reason for immediate despair, but rather for energy and determination to ward off the tide for as long as possible. The lesson he derived from events on the continent - in Geneva, in France and in the Netherlands - was that those who despaired and tried to conciliate were quickly overwhelmed. 'For God's sake', he wrote, 'let us shew a little firmness before we sacrifice one by one every political advantage that has been contributed to make this a great and dignified country'. (16) That his colleagues were fully in agreement with this firmness is demonstrated by the harsh sensitivity with which they reacted to the slightest sign of disaffection at home. In the wider conflict of the 1790s it was Grenville's strength of purpose against all the odds combined with his undying patriotism that held the ministry on course in the darkest moments of the war. Pitt's contribution was much less his determination than his shrewd political management and superb oratory, neither of which Grenville could remotely match. Grenville provided the hard core and Pitt the public face of the British war effort.

How to secure a counter-revolutionary settlement, however, was more than simply a question of national determination to strive for it. Britain's experiences with the counter-revolutionaries of revolutionised Europe were uniformly disappointing. In 1793-4 and in 1799-1800, the royalists of western France showed that they lacked the ability to achieve anything by themselves. Events at Toulon in 1793 and at Quiberon in 1795 showed that a small British military presence could not sustain them. And even the presence of the 40,000-strong Anglo-Russian army in Holland in 1799 failed to inspire the Dutch Orangists to revolt. There were other problems too. There was no guarantee that French royalists, any more than French republicans, were prepared to accept the territorial settlement which Britain had in mind. They were divided amongst themselves between ultras and constitutional royalists, each of whom developed their own organisations within France which conspired against each other and over which the British government had no real control. The British envoy in Piedmont, John Trevor, lamented in 1795 that

> they all wish to get our money, they all affect to load us with compliments for honour, generosity and

munificence, they flatter us with plans of counter-revolution...., but I am afraid the fact is that however they hate one another, they all in the bottom detest us. (17)

Attempts were made to overcome these obstacles. Grenville sent William Wickham to Switzerland in 1794 to make contact with the counter-revolutionaries and achieve a greater control over their efforts. Realising the disadvantages which would accrue from the royalists entering a defeated France on the coat-tails of the allies, ministers then subsidised Condé's émigré army in 1795 to spearhead an Austrian advance into south-eastern France, while Wickham organised a train of royalist revolt ahead of it, from the Franche-Comté through Lyons, right down to Marseille. With Wickham's financial backing, Condé managed to win over the commander of one of France's main Rhine armies, General Pichegru, while Wickham's agents also purchased the support of other commanders along the invasion route. But yet again the royalists could not manage things by themselves. They needed the backing of the Austrian army for Condé even to make a start, and this, because of the Polish crisis, was not forthcoming.

Again in 1797 Wickham spent £10,000 backing a scheme to secure a royalist majority in the French elections only to find that he could make very little use of the advantage thus gained because the mastermind of the whole enterprise, d'André, then had to admit that he dared not lead the deputies too openly in a pro-British line because then he would be lost: he could only try, he maintained, 'any line that can be taken, or any arguments that can be used, with a reasonable appearance of fairness and without shocking too openly the national prejudice ... which still exists in full force against the English nation'. (18) In the end, moreover, this scheme collapsed too because of the military weakness of the royalists - the Directory brought in the army to crush them in the coup d'état of Fructidor.

Ultimately therefore, the British government was no more successful with schemes of counter-revolutionary subversion in France than - as Dr Marianne Elliott makes clear below - the French government was with its schemes for promoting revolutionary subversion in Britain. The armed forces of counter-revolution in France might be used as a distraction and diversion to the Revolutionary armies, and Britain was very willing to supply arms and money in order to encourage such resistance (though the amounts of money were considerably less than the far from outstanding sums which it gave its allies). (19) But on the whole the most value achieved from cooperation with the French counter-revolution was in securing intelligence through the various royalist organisations. Even then the value was limited. The royalists always fed back overly-optimistic reports of the state of France. Although they got much closer to the French government than did French agents to the British, it is hard to see that the royalists fed back any useful intelligence about French plans that might have changed the course of the war. Their most reliable information was in the naval intelligence sent back through the Channel Islands correspondence and in the daily newspapers which they posted to London.

From 1796, the British began to pay the exiled Louis XVIII a pension, but it was difficult to see how it could put him back on his throne when he made unbending declarations (such as the hyper-reactionary Verona Declaration of 1796) that vitiated British efforts to achieve a union of the various shades of royalists within France; when the royalists quarrelled amongst themselves and were manifestly unable to help themselves; and when the French so manifestly detested anything to do with Britain. As the Anglo-French conflict progressed, the chances of a royalist restoration, rather than increasing, in fact decreased markedly. It was only a month before Napoleon's fall that the allies at last thought that they detected enough signs of pro-royalist sentiment within France to lead them to give full support for the return of the Bourbons.

In the light of the considerations outlined above, it might well be asked, not why it took so long for Britain to achieve its ends, but rather how it ever managed to achieve them at all. It signally failed to do so in the 1790s, and ended up on the worse side of a drawn peace in 1802. That Britain came out so well eventually and achieved a spectacularly successful peace settlement in 1814-5 was primarily due to the efforts of one man. That man was not Pitt, nor Grenville, nor Castlereagh, architects though all were of the terms of the final peace: the man was Napoleon Bonaparte. The propagandists of the Directory and of the Consulate had achieved considerable success in exploiting continental fears of excessive British power, so as to reduce participation in and to break up the coalitions created by Britain in the 1790s. As Emperor, however, Napoleon was unwilling to restrain his ambitions long enough to allow this European-wide resentment to mature. His expansive designs and his complementary efforts to hold Europe in line against Britain by force eventually convinced the continental powers that Napoleonic France presented an immediate threat to their political viability far greater than Britain presented to their long-term commercial interests. Even then they were reluctant to destroy him outright: Napoleon destroyed himself, and paved the way for the restoration of the Bourbons, by refusing all the compromise terms of peace that the allies offered him in 1813 and in early 1814. His own intransigence forced the allies to play the British game, and they took Britain's money in an all-out effort to crush him, when even up to a few weeks of the end of the war in April 1814 few in Britain would have dared to predict that they were at last on the brink of achieving almost all that they had striven for over the previous quarter of a century.

Postscript

In the final peace settlement of 1814-5, Britain established its maritime security by obtaining Tobago and Saint Lucia in the West Indies and Mauritius in the Indian Ocean. France had the rest of its former West Indian empire restored to it, but Martinique and Guadeloupe were by then very run down and Saint-Domingue was to all intents and purposes impossible to recover from the rebel slaves, so that there seemed little likelihood of French commercial recovery in the near future. Britain additionally ensured its maritime security and strengthened its commerce by retaining the Cape, Ceylon, Demerara and Essequibo (British Guiana) from Holland, and Trinidad from Spain, – thus consolidating both its

West and East Indian empires. As regards <u>continental security</u>, France
was pushed back to its 1790 frontiers, Belgium was joined to Holland,
Prussia acquired territory in the Rhineland, and Austria was
strengthened in Italy as buffers to possible French expansion, the whole
being guaranteed by a mutual defence pact among the Great Powers (the
Quadruple Alliance). The latter impeded British <u>isolationism</u>, but
<u>counter-revolution</u> was asserted anew, especially through the restoration
of the Bourbons in France and Spain and the House of Orange in the new
kingdom of the Netherlands.

Notes

1. Pitt was succeeded temporarily in 1801 by Addington who brought the
Revolutionary War to a close in 1802 only to resume conflict again with
Napoleon just over a year later.

2. British Library, Department of Manuscripts, Loan 57/107: Dundas to
the Duke of Richmond, 8 July 1793.

3. Idem.

4. Bodleian Library, Oxford, Bland Burges manuscripts, 'Transcripts of
political papers of ... Sir James Burges, 1789-92, 1814-6', f. 75:
Burges to Lord Auckland, 17 March 1792.

5. <u>Memoirs of the Court and Cabinets of George III</u>, ed. Duke of
Buckingham and Chandos (4 vols., London, 1853-5), II, pp. 221-5.

6. William Clements Library, Ann Arbor, Michigan, Pitt Papers: Pitt to
Dundas, 15 November 1792.

7. This summary of British policy as regards a restoration is based on
the Declarations of 29 October and 20 November 1793 (in <u>The
Parliamentary History of England</u>, XXX (London, 1817), cols. 1057-61;
Grenville's correspondence with Pitt relating to the administration of
Toulon (Public Record Office, PRO 30/8/140, PRO 30/8/334); and
Grenville's instructions to his envoys Eden (FO 7/34, 7 September 1793),
St.Helens (FO 72/28, 4, 22 October 1793), Wickham (<u>Correspondence of
William Wickham</u>, 2 vols., London, 1870, I, pp. 12-14), and Macartney (FO
27/45 10 July 1795); and Sir Gilbert Elliot's conversations with
ministers (National Library of Scotland, Minto Papers, M 453, Journal
entry 8 September 1793).

8. British Library, Loan 57/107: to Richmond, 8 July 1793.

9. Public Record Office, FO 7/60, Minto to Grenville, 7 September 1800;
FO 64/58, Carysfort to Grenville, 27 September 1800.

10. <u>British Diplomacy, 1813-5</u>, ed. C.K. Webster, London, 1921, pp. 74,
127, 147, 153.

11. <u>Parl. Hist. of England</u>, XXX, col. 378.

12. J.M. Sherwig, <u>Guineas and gunpowder. British foreign aid in the wars</u> <u>with France, 1793-1815</u>, Cambridge, Mass., 1969, pp. 37, 181-2, 365-8.

13. France, <u>Archives des affaires étrangères</u>, Correspondance politique: Angleterre 595: 'Coup d'oeil politique sur l'Angleterre', 4 Floréal an IX, f. 15 v. The classic poetic exposition of this spirit is Wordsworth's ode, <u>November 1806</u>.

14. <u>Parl. Hist of England</u>, XXX, cols. 1017, 1282-5.

15. <u>Wickham Corresp.</u>, II, p. 6.

16. Scottish Record Office, Melville Castle Muniments, GD 51/1/528(1): Grenville to Dundas, 16 August 1797; <u>Court and Cabinets</u>, II, p. 306.

17. Public Record Office, FO 67/16: Trevor to Grenville, 11 April 1795.

18. W.R. Fryer, <u>Republic or restoration in France? 1794-7</u>, Manchester, 1965, p. 285.

19. There is no single account of the money spent by the British government in support of the counter-revolution. The biggest single payment was the c. £824,000 spent on the émigré army of Condé, serving with the Austrian army in Germany, between 1795 and 1797 (see Public Record Office, FO 74/37), but while ministers had its potential usefulness to the counter-revolution in mind, they also regarded it as part of their contribution to the Austrian war effort. Total British secret service expenditure during the period 1792-1801 was approximately 1.2 millions on <u>all</u> purposes internal and external. Much of this was for normal information-gathering purposes rather than for sponsoring counter-revolution, and the most obvious direct payments towards the counter-revolution in France were the £78,000 to the royalists in western France provided by Windham between 1795 and 1797 and the greater part of the total secret service expenditure of Wickham and his successor Talbot of £303,000 between 1795 and 1799. Money was also given to the royalist agency in London managed by Dutheil, but this does not seem to have been considerable, while Louis XVIII himself was paid 3,000 in 1796, £9,000 in 1797, £5,000 over the period from January to May 1798 and £500 per month from June of the same year. Altogether <u>direct</u> assistance to the opponents of the government within France would seem to have been nearer £500,000 than £1 million. H. Mitchell, <u>The underground war against Revolutionary France</u>, Oxford, 1965, pp. 256-60 (the writer differs from Mitchell's conclusions); <u>Historical Manuscripts Commission. Manuscripts of J.B. Fortescue preserved at Dropmore</u>, London, 1892-1927, II, p. 363; Public Records Office, Audit Office 1/2121, Roll 5; British Library, Additional Manuscripts 37,844.
    In the War of American Independence, France gave £457,000 in subsidies and £1,522,000 in loans between 1777 and 1783 to the American rebels against the British government (S.F. Bernis, <u>A diplomatic history of the United States</u>, New York, 1965, p. 24, converting French <u>livres</u> at 23 to £1).

The Anglo-French Conflict in the Caribbean in the 1790's

DAVID GEGGUS

The West Indies in the eighteenth century were the most valuable and most vulnerable parts of the French and British colonial empires. Britain's Caribbean colonies accounted for about one-fifth of Britain's overseas trade during the 1780s, and throughout the century they were Britain's most important trading partners outside Europe. The French West Indies were even more important to their mother country, generating some two-thirds of France's foreign trade, and by 1789 they were producing nearly half of the world's sugar and well over half the world's coffee. Enormous sums of capital were tied up in the Caribbean, in land, sugar factories and, above all, slaves, of whom the British colonies possessed (in 1790) 480,000 and the French about 675,000.

Not surprisingly, the West Indian colonies were prime targets in almost every European war. Each side wanted to deprive the other of its commerce and perhaps make valuable additions to its empire, though few settled colonies actually changed hands. Fleets were usually rushed out to the Caribbean at the beginning of a war, and the smaller islands were frequently occupied by enemy forces, to be haggled over afterwards at the conference table. Warfare in the West Indies was invariably costly, both in money and in human life. Tropical fevers could be expected to carry off thousands of soldiers and seamen in each campaign.

What, then, was different about the conflict in the 1790s, the penultimate Anglo-French war in the Caribbean? In many respects, it differed only in scale from previous conflicts. The prizes fought over were more valuable than ever; the forces engaged were larger, and the losses consequently greater. There was perhaps more controversy than in the American and Seven Years' Wars surrounding the merits of a Caribbean offensive: attitudes towards colonies were changing. There was, however, a truly revolutionary dimension to the struggle with the French Republic, in the Caribbean even more than in Europe.

Slavery and chains were merely metaphors in European politics. In the West Indies, they were facts of everyday life. The French

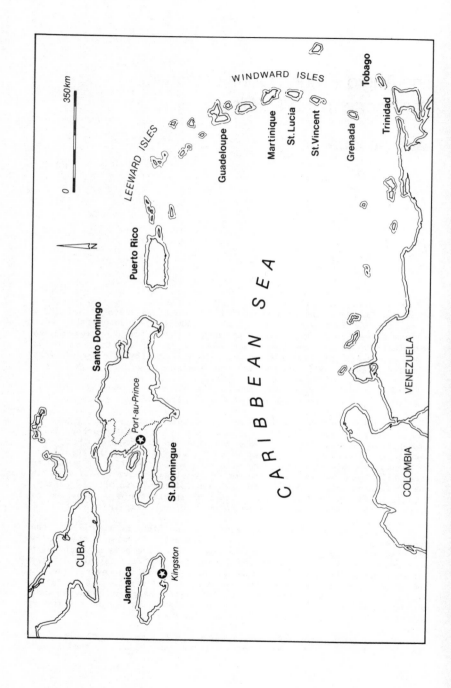

Revolution brought a threat to the social order of the Caribbean
unparalleled elsewhere, and with it a counter-revolution that seemed to
promise rich and easy pickings for the enemies of France. The break
with the conventional wars of the eighteenth century, profound enough in
Europe, was at its most dramatic in the West Indies.

1. The French West Indies and the Revolution.

In order of economic significance, France's possessions in the West
Indies were Saint Domingue (modern Haiti), Guadeloupe, Martinique and
Saint Lucia, and included several smaller islands. By far the most
important was Saint Domingue, which was entirely in a class of its own.
Although little larger than Wales, its total production was roughly
double that of all the British West Indies put together. Its slave
population of some half a million blacks was the largest and fastest-
growing in the Caribbean, and its 8,000 plantations made it probably the
wealthiest colony in the world. (1)

Despite this disparity between Saint Domingue and the other
colonies, they were all similar in social structure. Their white
communities were always tiny minorities, usually less than one-tenth of
the total population. They were united by racial solidarity, but
divided by class tensions that tended to oppose sugar and coffee
planters, lawyers and merchants, and to separate all of these from the
turbulent petits blancs who were poor whites varying from plantation
overseers to artisans, shopkeepers, seamen and pedlars. Slightly less
numerous were the free coloureds. They were freed slaves and the
descendants of freed slaves, and very often of mixed racial descent.
Generally speaking, they functioned as a colonial middle class,
competing with the petits blancs though they covered a broad economic
spectrum and, in Saint Domingue, included many wealthy and educated
planters. They were all, however, subjected to humiliating race laws,
as well as informal harassment, especially from poor whites. Resented
by the slaves and rejected by the whites, the position of the free
coloureds was profoundly ambiguous. At the base of colonial society,
and the source of its wealth, were the slaves. On long-settled
Martinique and perhaps Guadeloupe too, most slaves were creoles, that is
island-born and raised in slavery. In Saint Domingue, however, the
majority were Africans who had arrived manacled in the holds of
slaveships. In the late 1780s, they were being imported into the colony
at a rate of over 30,000 a year.

The revolution in Paris threw the French West Indies into chaos.
While exacerbating social and political tensions, it gradually
undermined, or destroyed outright the traditional sources of power in
the islands (Governor, Intendant, law courts, garrison, militia,
police). In the three main colonies the white communities split into
warring factions, and the free coloureds demanded political equality,
eventually taking up arms to make good their claims. And then, in
August 1791, the slaves of Saint Domingue's opulent North Province rose
in revolt and with firebrands and machetes took a terrible revenge on
their white masters. The greatest slave revolt of all time, involving
around 100,000 slaves, it did not spread to the South and West Provinces

of Saint Domingue, although during the next two years they, too, were the scene of spasmodic uprisings and of civil war between the whites and the free coloureds.

France's Revolutionary politicians were extremely embarrassed by events in the Caribbean and the issues they raised – colonial self-government, racial equality and human freedom, on the one hand, and national prosperity on the other. There was a great reluctance to tamper with the colonial status quo, but by 1792 full equality was finally granted to the free coloureds, who were needed to fight the slaves.

This concession did much to alienate the white colonists from France. Age-old desires for political autonomy and free trade were now powerfully reinforced. The small minority of whites who had harboured secessionist designs (especially since the American Revolution) now grew in number. Of these, some favoured independence; others, rule by Great Britain. The British planters' tradition of self-government was envied in the French Caribbean, as was their cheaper, more plentiful supply of slaves and the naval protection the colonies received in wartime. Once the slave revolt had broken out – and it was universally blamed on metropolitan interference – British rule became all the more attractive. Troops were needed and substantial credit, which Revolutionary France was in no position to supply. Overtures were now made to the British government, though without success.

When the French monarchy was overthrown in August 1792, this autonomist strand in Dominguan politics, apparently a policy of middling, resident planters, came to be reinforced by a royalist, counter-revolutionary strand, which drew support from colonists with a military background and resonant titles, often absentees. This tendency was most pronounced in the Windward Isles (Martinique and Guadeloupe), which immediately seceded once the Republic was declared.

At the beginning of 1793, when war between Britain and France was imminently expected, planters from both Saint Domingue and the Windwards came to London and formally proposed that British forces occupy their colonies and save them from the newly-formed alliance of Republicans and free coloureds. The status of the colonies would remain undecided until the peace, though meanwhile the colonists were to swear allegiance to the British crown. Accommodating many shades of opinion, this was an act of secession, counter-revolution and self-preservation all at the same time.

2. The British reaction to the Revolution.

Jamaica, the largest and most prosperous of the British colonies, could be reached from Saint Domingue by canoe. To the Jamaican planters, therefore, the garish images of revolt that filtered through from the French colony in the autumn of 1791 must have seemed like the enactment of their very worst nightmare: slave armies with guns and cannon, hundreds of plantations ablaze, white captives hung up with hooks through their chins, men sawn in half, children impaled. Within a

few days of the news reaching Kingston, Jamaican slaves were singing
songs about the rebellion and swaggering in the streets of the capital.
The slaves were now, someone wrote from Kingston,
        so different a people from what they were ... that I am
        convinced that the ideas of liberty have sunk so deep in
        the minds of all negroes, that whenever the greatest
        precautions are not taken, they will rise'. (2)
White Jamaica went into a convulsion of defensive activity and clamoured
for troops to be sent out from England.

        Just how seriously the government took the threat of race war in
the Caribbean is not entirely clear. Financial cuts were then the order
of the day and ministers actually wanted to reduce the size of the
already large West Indian garrisons. Extra regiments were eventually
sent out, but only after the planters had agreed to pay for them. After
all, slave revolts had not been particularly rare in the West Indies and
none had lasted very long. The ministry tended to see the revolt in
European perspective. The French economy had been seriously damaged.
Therefore Britain might look forward to a long period of peace. Despite
fears of further stirring up the slaves in the Caribbean, plans also
went ahead for the abolition of the slave trade from Africa. However,
like other measures of liberal reform, these soon fell foul of the fear
of Jacobinism and the increasingly conservative climate that set in
during the latter half of 1792.

        So much for the perceived dangers of the Saint Domingue slave
revolt. Perhaps more apparent at the time were the benefits it brought,
both potential political advantage and immediate commercial gain. The
destruction of the prosperous northern plain of Saint Domingue left a
large hole in the world market for tropical produce and prices went sky
high. British planters cleared new land for sugar and coffee, as a boom
began that would last throughout the 1790s. At the same time, the
Revolution was progressively disrupting France's colonial trade and
British merchants were stepping in to take over a sizeable share of, in
particular, the cotton and indigo trades. Lord Hawkesbury, the
President of the Board of Trade, noted the great gains that British
commerce would make if the whites of Saint Domingue made themselves
independent or sought a foreign protectorate. Even if the blacks were
to win, he thought, Britain would considerably benefit through the
destruction of a rival, though it would be at the peril of her own
colonies.

        Prime Minister Pitt was then immersed in projects of financial
reform, but like Hawkesbury he recognised that the future of Saint
Domingue would be very important to Great Britain. In November 1791, he
granted two interviews with the Dominguan radical planter, Venault de
Charmilly. Something of a visionary, Charmilly wanted the British to
promote the secession not only of Saint Domingue but of all the colonies
of South America as well. Among the British public officials who wanted
to see Britain profit from this secessionist movement in the French
colonies were the Governor of Jamaica and the British Ambassador in
Paris. Pitt, however, and the Foreign Secretary, Grenville, refused to
countenance any sort of interference, beyond changing the laws of trade
to admit French sugar and coffee into British ports for re-export. Only

when war with France became a real possibility, in December 1792, did ministers and planters begin a cautious dialogue, and Pitt, to the frustration of many, refused to enter into any agreement until war had actually been declared. Whether the prospect of Caribbean spoils made the ministry more willing to go to war, as the Opposition suggested, it seems difficult to say.

3. War policy in 1793.

Historians have tended to disagree as to how important was the Caribbean in the government's war policy, and as to whether its Caribbean strategy is best described as defensive or aggressive. The ministry's priorities in the first months of hostilities are certainly unclear. It may be that none were formulated and the government merely responded to changing circumstances. Pitt had been forced into a war he did not want and then had to start improvising.

With the armed forces run down to a very low level, it was apparently thought that little could be achieved in the West Indies until new regiments were raised and an expedition sent out in the autumn. This was the usual time for such expeditions to sail, after the summer 'hurricane months' but in time for the relatively dry and healthy winter. The 6,000 soldiers already in the West Indies were deemed sufficient for colonial defence, and they were authorised at the outbreak of war to attempt to occupy the French Windwards, should no resistance be anticipated. It was to be a cut-price campaign, aimed at collecting windfalls, and initially this was as far as the government was prepared to go. Then in June, Jamaican forces were authorised to attempt a landing in Saint Domingue as well, and in July a divided Cabinet approved the plan for an autumn expedition. By this time, the Flanders campaign had become the government's main priority, and when the expedition was assembled in October it was delayed by fresh developments in the war in Europe and over a third of its complement was diverted to the Breton coast. It finally set sail on November 25th, with little more than 6,000 men.

Curiously, the French Windwards were to be the expedition's main target, possibly for logistical reasons, or perhaps they were thought militarily easier options, or even more valuable, having suffered less destruction. Whatever the reasons, it is clear that the ministry was thinking in terms of aggrandisement and not defence. Otherwise it would have concentrated on strife-torn Saint Domingue. 'Indemnity for the past and security for the future' were Pitt's declared aims. Even Henry Dundas, the chief proponent of the Caribbean strategy, had to admit that campaigns in Europe might be more effective in bringing down the French Republic. Since France's colonial trade was already ruined, there could be no pretence of trying to weaken her war effort economically. However, this is not to say that Dundas was lying when, in later years, he would insist that it was a 'war for security' and not a 'war for riches'. As will be seen, ministerial motives and the situation in the Caribbean were to change dramatically in the first eighteen months of fighting.

4. Early successes.

At the outbreak of war, British forces in the Caribbean were outnumbered by the French, especially at sea, and consequently little was achieved. In retrospect, we can see that Britain's delay in taking action in the West Indies was to prove fatal. The Republicans took control of the Windwards with free coloured help in December 1792, and in the next six months they suppressed two uprisings by royalist planters who were anticipating British help. A half-hearted and nervous British landing in June became a fiasco and was rapidly abandoned amid mutual recriminations. This failure to co-ordinate activities on both sides of the Atlantic further worsened relations between clamourous planters on one hand and a mistrustful military and haughty ministers on the other. It was also said to have caused the execution or dispossession of 6,000 colonists. More seriously, however, the threat of intervention in Saint Domingue drove the Republic's Civil Commissioners into the desperate act, in August 1793, of freeing and arming the slaves. Though no one could foresee it at the time, in Saint Domingue as in France, it was the levée en masse that was to save the Republic.

Meanwhile, however, British policy began to yield results. Six hundred soldiers from Jamaica occupied several remote parts of Saint Domingue and were welcomed by the planters. In March and April 1794, General Grey's expedition captured the French Windwards after brief, hard-fought campaigns, and he then sent on troops to Saint Domingue. They arrived in time to capture the capital, Port au Prince, and celebrate there on 6 June the birthday of George III. This was to be the high-point of the British campaign in the Caribbean.

5. The Revolution spreads.

Already, however, as soon as the spring rains started to fall, troops began to sicken and die in large numbers. Crowded into the seaports, they fell victim to devastating epidemics of yellow fever, to which their enemies were immune and which killed up to two-thirds of some regiments in a couple of months. By the end of the year, desperately depleted garrisons were hanging on for their lives in the occupied colonies.

Meanwhile, the task of maintaining or reviving the slave regime had become enormously more difficult. In February 1794, the French Convention in effect ratified the actions of its Commissioners in Saint Domingue and, amidst great emotion, declared slavery abolished in all French colonies. An epoch-making decision, it probably owed less to Jacobin ideology than to the threat of imminent English conquest of France's colonial empire.
> By casting loose liberty in the New World, [declared
> Danton] it will yield abundant fruit .... Pitt and his
> cronies shall be swept away into oblivion.... C'est
> aujourd'hui que l'Anglais est mort!' (3)

The emancipation decree did bear fruit almost immediately in both

Saint Domingue and Guadeloupe. Henceforth, the blacks' skills as
guerilla fighters and their familiarity with climate and terrain would
be combined with the naval, military and financial resources of a
European state. In Saint Domingue, the emancipation decree was probably
the main element in the cementing of a crucial alliance between the
Republic and the brilliant black leader, Toussaint Louverture. A
general and politician of great skill, he had moulded together out of
the fieldhands and flunkeys of the slave plantations a disciplined army
of guerilla fighters about 4,000 strong. His rallying to the French in
the spring of 1794 is rightly considered the turning point in the
Haitian Revolution.

At the same time, there landed in Guadeloupe a small force sent out
from France under a West Indian-born Jacobin, Victor Hugues. He
emancipated the slaves, executed his royalist prisoners and, by the end
of the year, had driven the British off the island. At sea, using all
kinds of vessels from sloops to canoes, he launched a privateering war,
which had a devastating effect on British commerce. Even more
disturbing for the British, Victor Hugues also began a secret war
against their own colonies. Agents were sent to try and foment
rebellion among the non-white population and propaganda tracts were
distributed along with tricolour cockades (which were sometimes regarded
as amulets or talismans). These agents were usually multi-lingual free
coloureds and were landed from small boats or were sent via the United
States. Particular objects for their attention were potentially
dissident groups, such as the Black Caribs of Saint Vincent, the
Jamaican Maroons (free descendants of runaway slaves) and French
prisoners of war.

The British were horrified by such activity. Victor Hugues was
soon known as the 'colonial Robespierre', and his exploits regularly
appear in British correspondance as 'savage' or 'diabolical' —
adjectives that in fact far better describe the treatment of black
prisoners by Britain's planter allies. The spectacle of ex-slaves
winning battles shocked political sensibilities and offended racial
prejudice. It also posed a grave threat to the British economy and
caused considerable alarm among financiers, merchants and planters.
Henry Dundas complained of the French Republic's 'extraordinary and
unprecedented system' of waging war. By the end of the year, defence
had become the government's main concern in the Carribean.

During the first half of 1795, British fears were fully realised,
when revolution and race war spread to the British islands of Grenada
and Saint Vincent and the occupied colony of Saint Lucia, where the
British forces were driven out in June. When the Maroon War broke out
in Jamaica the following month, many concluded that the French were out
to subvert the New World.

6. The Abercromby expedition.

In the West Indies, the British now turned reluctantly to fighting
the French with their own weapons. Small ships were fitted out locally
to fight the privateers, and by an extraordinary irony, 'black

regiments' were recruited among the slaves with promises of freedom. In all, twelve were raised in the British islands, as well as many ephemeral corps in the occupied French colonies. Most planters bitterly resisted the experiment, but it proved in general highly succcessful and substantially reduced the number of white troops needed to garrison the West Indies. However, to reconquer the ground lost to the Republicans, greatest hope was pinned on a massive new expedition to be sent out from England.

During the summer of 1795, Dundas put together with remarkable energy a force of over 30,000 soldiers and more than 200 ships, then the largest expedition ever assembled in Great Britain. The countryside around Southampton and Cork blazed with red uniforms, as bell tents mushroomed row upon row in farmers' fields. Hundreds of tons of stores converged upon the two ports, and heavy-laden ordnance ships winched aboard cannon and shot at the wharves of Woolwich arsenal. The expedition was placed under the command of Sir Ralph Abercromby, the most respected general of the day.

In Parliament, the Whigs complained that the country was being left defenceless against a French invasion, but Dundas successfully argued that, having been driven from the Continent, Britain's priority should now be the Caribbean. Spain's withdrawal from the war in July and sudden friendship with France had both increased the danger to Britain's colonies and held out the prospect of fresh conquests of largely virgin territory. The undefended Dutch colonies were similarly tempting. The Admiralty had been hostile to offensive operations in the West Indies, but this hostility ended with the appointment of the colonially-minded Lord Spencer as First Sea Lord.

The expedition was meticulously prepared and, though it encountered many mishaps in being assembled, it still managed to sail in November, at an earlier date than any previous force for the West Indies. It was unfortunate for the men concerned that the years 1794-6 were a period of freak winter gales of great severity. For months the ships battled with the fury of the elements and many were sunk, hundreds of bodies being washed ashore along the south coast. Not till February did the expedition, much depleted, manage to clear the British Isles.

Another campaign season was thus lost in the West Indies, and the troops, much weakened by the voyage, died like flies on reaching the Caribbean. Nevertheless, after several difficult campaigns in jungle and mountain terrain, the British West Indies were finally made secure and Saint Lucia reconquered. Spanish Trinidad and Dutch Demerara were also taken at little cost. The war in Saint Domingue, by contrast, went on getting more and more expensive, and the activities of the Guadeloupe privateers reached a new intensity in the period 1796-8.

7. Military life.

The central experience of the soldier's life in the Caribbean was without doubt death from disease. Over half of the troops sent out to the West Indies died there. A soldier who survived a year in Saint

Domingue usuallly saw six or seven out of every ten of his comrades
perish. Fear of being sent to the West Indies made recruiting for the
Army a difficult task and, along with the huge wartime expansion in the
armed forces, this helps explain why military standards in these years
sank to such a low level. Most of the regiments that crossed the
Atlantic were newly-raised, half-trained and without discipline or
esprit de corps. Of these, the worst were sent to Saint Domingue.

Manchester mill-hands, Lincolnshire labourers, Irish and German
peasants, however novel for them was the experience of becoming a
soldier, their introduction to the West Indies must have been even more
dramatic. Towering mountains and lush vegetation, a violent climate and
a bizarre population, these were the soldier's first impressions as he
was drawn into a world of savage conflict where death assumed the most
terrifying forms and on a scale of incredible senselessness. Surrounded
by an exotic enemy, hydra-like and elusive, numbering tens of thousands,
the troops were often unable to set foot beyond their picket lines
without being sniped at or ambushed. As their numbers dwindled,
military duties fell the more heavily on the survivors. Consequently,
men went for months without taking off their clothes for a full night's
sleep. The ease with which men became fatigued or fainted probably owed
much to their tight-fitting, woollen uniforms, caked with sweat, and to
their tendency not to wash.

As few regiments managed to arrive in the dry season, it was never
very long before new arrivals were struck down with malaria or yellow
fever. The effect could be devastating. Men fit in the morning were
sometimes dead by nightfall. Two weeks after disembarking in Saint
Domingue, a bewildered officer was writing, 'Hundreds almost were
absolutely drowned in their own blood, bursting from them at every pore.
Some died raving mad, others forming plans of attacking, others
desponding'. (4) At Port au Prince, the great wards of the General
Hospital were packed with the victims of yellow fever, whose groans and
stench made the building a nightmare to experience. As death
approached, the patient would throw up large quantities of digested
blood, the fearful 'black vomit'. He became incontinent; his nose would
often bleed and haemorrhaging might also occur from the corners of the
eyes. Some men, delirious, tried to leap out of the windows. Others,
tragically, remained clear of mind until death.

Trapped between the mountains and the sea and poisoned, so it
seemed, by the very air they had to breathe, troops of all ranks found
an escape through drunkenness. Officers and men could daily be found in
a drunken stupor. Although it was an age of alcoholic excess, the tales
of troops filling their canteens with rum before campaigns or smuggling
alcohol into their messes, and into the hospitals, suggest an obsession
born of desperate circumstances. In the folk medicine of the day,
moreover, alcohol was regarded as a prophylactic against and as a cure
for fever - fire to drive out fire. This is of more than passing
interest, for hepatic or renal failure is the usual cause of death in
yellow fever, which is not normally a high fatality disease. Along with
general debility, multiple infection and heroically inept medical
treatment, overdrinking must be accounted one of the major causes of the
high mortality rates of these epidemics. This is why the matter of

regimental discipline was so important.

For British troops, this was mainly a war of posts and ambushes, apart from a few formal assaults and sieges in 1794. Colonial troops sometimes conducted raids, but the Europeans usually fought on the defensive behind fortifications. Battle casualties were remarkably few, although among the ex-slaves losses were enormous. When attacking, the blacks displayed a bravery that was only too often suicidal.

This was both a race war and a civil war. While the colonists had never treated rebellious blacks with anything but savagery, they themselves were regarded by the French Republic as traitors to their country. The slave-owners were fighting for their survival as a class; the blacks, for their freedom. Quarter was rarely given on either side, and the planters often mistreated their prisoners. The British tended to disapprove but acquiesce: salutary neglect, it was doubtless thought.

8. The reaction in Britain.

Back in England, the obituary columns were littered with the names of men who had died in the West Indies. Burke railed against fighting to conquer a cemetery, and the Whigs kept demanding to know the cost of the campaigns. Almost every person in the country, it was claimed in Parliament, had lost an acquaintance in the Caribbean. Men were refusing to enlist and some said the nation's safety was endangered. In May 1797, the Whigs forced a debate, demanding that the troops be withdrawn from Saint Domingue. The ministry had given up any hopes of conquest but feared the effect such a reversal would have on its slave colonies. The motion was easily defeated. Even so, the costs of occupation remained unacceptably high, and the local commander, Thomas Maitland, favoured withdrawal. Dramatic advances by Toussaint Louverture finally clinched the matter, and the surviving troops were eventually evacuated in September 1798.

At the same time, the Directory recalled Victor Hugues to France and the Caribbean ceased to be a major theatre of operations, though in the three years before the peace of Amiens more Dutch and Danish colonies were occupied without resistance. The government's main concern in this period was the increasing power and independence of Toussaint Louverture, who was turning Saint Domingue into an autonomous black state. Would he launch a war of liberation in the West Indies? How would slaves elsewhere react? While most Europeans looked on with horrid fascination, the British cultivated good relations with Toussaint, signing a non-aggression pact and trading to their mutual advantage. As long as hostilities with France persisted, the uncomfortable spectacle of black power in a former slave colony had to be tolerated. However, once Bonaparte came to power and a European peace was in sight, the possibility of French aggression in the West Indies became the lesser of two evils. In October 1801, five months before peace was signed, a French expedition sailed for the reconquest of Saint Domingue with the blessing of the Addington government.

9. The cost of the campaigns.

During the 1790s, more than 60,000 British soldiers were sent out to the Caribbean to join the 6,000 already stationed there. At least 7,000 foreign troops in British pay also served with them. Both contemporaries and modern historians have tended to exaggerate the losses that they suffered. During the first six years of the war, these were approximately as follows:

TABLE 1. Losses of British troops in the Caribbean, 1793-98.

	DEAD	DISCHARGED	DESERTED	TOTAL
South Caribbean	19,055	4,100	545	23,700
Jamaica	2,990	1,395	680	5,065
Saint Domingue	12,695	1,410	300	14,405
TOTAL	34,740	6,905	1,525	43,170

TABLE 2. Losses of foreign regiments in British pay, 1793-98.

	DEAD	DISCHARGED	DESERTED	TOTAL
South Caribbean	3,240	155	140	3,535
Saint Domingue	2,500	100?	200?	2,800?
TOTAL	5,740	255	340	6,335

Losses of seamen are much harder to estimate, but tentatively might be put at around 10,000 dead. Total British losses, therefore, probably did not exceed 60,000. Of course, soldiers did not stop dying in the West Indies in 1798. By the time peace was signed in 1802, at least another 5,000 had been buried there. The financial cost of the campaigns, leaving aside expenditure on the Royal Navy, came to around 16 million pounds sterling in the period 1793-8.

Both in blood and treasure, warfare in the West Indies was extremely costly, because of logistical problems, official corruption and disease. However, much of the cost incurred would have arisen anyway, had the government mounted a Caribbean offensive or not. The British West Indies still had to be defended. And men could die of malaria in the Low Countries as well as in the West Indies where, however, they at least did not freeze to death. Because of the ministry's greater commitment of troops to the Continent in the earlier part of the war, the difference in cost between the Caribbean and Continental campaigns was not all that great. The idea that Britain's war effort was fatally weakened by the intervention in Saint Domingue, or even by the West Indies expeditions in general, will not bear examination.

Furthermore, a sizeable part of the cost of offensive operations in the Caribbean was recouped directly in taxation, as well as indirectly through stimulating trade. Even the benighted British administration in Saint Domingue managed to collect nearly half a million pounds in local taxes, and doubtless rather more was raised in Martinique and Demerara.

In the years 1794-8, imports into Great Britain from just Martinique and Saint Domingue paid over £760,000 in customs duty, while the imports from Britain amounted to almost three and a half million pounds, more than one-fifth as much as those of the entire British West Indies. Demerara, occupied in 1796, became a much more important trading partner.

It might be said, of course, that the attempt to seize Saint Domingue (which absorbed over a third of the costs involved) was always doomed to failure and was, therefore, reckless – but this is by no means certain. All hinged on delivering a heavy blow early in the war. Without doubt, the diversion of troops to the Continent harmed the West Indies campaigns far more than those campaigns hindered the war effort in Europe. Moral considerations apart, therefore, the ministry's Caribbean strategy represented a sound attempt to extend Britain's tropical empire. Yet, it was their defensive aspect that ministers chose to stress when justifying the costs they entailed. Jamaica, they argued, would have been worth nothing if Saint Domingue had not been occupied. The argument certainly carried weight. Jamaica was then importing between one and two million pounds sterling worth of British produce each year, and British-grown sugar was generating between one and a half and two millions annually in customs revenue. Nevertheless, it does not follow that occupying enemy colonies was the best way of protecting these increasingly valuable assets. As regards Jamaica and Saint Domingue, a defensive strategy would probably have been more effective. However, with respect to the South Caribbean, the ministry's argument from necessity looks far more plausible.

Neither the Caribbean nor the Continental campaigns of the 1790s contributed anything to ending the war with France, and in human and financial terms both were extremely costly. West Indies operations, however, possessed a more positive fiscal, economic and defensive rationale than those in Europe, and their cost was considerably less than has been usually supposed.

Notes

1. For a recent survey of Saint-Dominique in the 1790s, see my Slavery, War and Revolution: the British Occupation of Saint Domingue 1793-98 (Oxford, 1982).

2. Public Record Office, CO 137/89 anonymous letter, 18 November 1791.

3. J. Morse Stephens, Speeches of the statesmen and orators of the French Revolution (Oxford, 1892), pp. 281-2.

4. Boston Public Library, Massachussetts, Lieutenant Howard's Journal, vol.1, pp. 61-2.

French Subversion in Britain in the French Revolution

MARIANNE ELLIOTT

The belief in a French-inspired conspiracy against established
governments everywhere was a popular one among the governing classes of
late eighteenth-century Europe and is best represented by the
influential treatise of the French émigré the Abbé Barruel, Mémoires
pour servir à l'histoire du jacobinisme, published in 1797. The claim
was already a favourite with successive British governments since the
outbreak of war with revolutionary France in 1793 and normally figured
in their justification of stringent security measures. Thus the various
reports from parliamentary secret committees on domestic subversion –
which usually prefaced a new batch of suppressive legislation – would
claim to have found 'the clearest proofs of a systematic design ... by
France, in conjunction with domestic traitors ... to overturn the laws,
constitution, and government ... both in Great Britain and Ireland ...'
(1799 report), or 'the fullest proofs that the dangerous and treasonable
conspiracy for the subversion of the constitution and government ... in
concert with a foreign enemy ... has never been abandoned'. (1801
report) (1) Such claims were dismissed by government detractors as
scare mongering, mere excuses for the perpetuation of emergency
legislation for most of the 1790s, and it was Francis Place who coined
the oft-used phrase Pitt's 'Reign of Terror' to describe the process.
The epithet is of course ridiculous and Gwyn Williams' still immensely
readable Artisans and Sans Culottes (1968) points the moral by comparing
the acquittal of Thomas Hardy by an English jury in 1794 with the fate
of those brought before the Revolutionary Tribunal in Paris. (2) In
another paper I have accepted that there was a good deal of exaggeration
of the threat on the part of government, particularly in its effort to
discredit the parliamentary opposition. (3) But the tendency to dismiss
government pronouncements as mere scare mongering can be (and was at the
time) carried too far, and may lead to the rejection altogether of the
existence of domestic conspiracy and foreign subversion. More recent
research has modified both approaches, and a better insight into the
workings of Britain's secret service shows that these parliamentary

reports, far from being the fabrications of popular myth or symbols of a credulous government duped by mercenary agents, were the products of careful detective work and the information of reliable secret agents.

The workings of French undercover activities in Britain during this decade still comprise, however, a neglected area of research; as a result several major areas of historical controversy remain highly speculative on this point, particularly the question of conspiracy or revolutionary rumblings in England during this period. It would be a brave historian who would claim that England was threatened with revolution in the 1790s, when the idea has been so decisively laid to rest by a whole succession of historians since the time of Halévy. But Edward Thompson's brilliant analysis in the 1960s of the formation of working-class consciousness, and subsequent research which has built on his conclusions, shows that at least an element of conspiratorial or subversive, if not always revolutionary, thinking, must be accepted as part of a developing radical tradition. My own research has shown that, whilst direct French subversion in Britain was erratic and never commanded the unanimous backing from Paris which British government statements implied, whilst the revolutionary underground in late eighteenth-century England was dwarfed by the surge of wartime loyalism, - and any suggestion that it was capable of organising internal revolution is preposterous - nevertheless the fears of government were well-founded: internal pockets of conspiracy did exist and derived their strength from their attachment to a much more powerful Irish revolutionary movement, and through it to a military alliance with revolutionary France. This argument I have developed elsewhere and the topic of particular concern here is the precise nature of French involvement in the promotion of disaffection on the British mainland. The conclusions I hope to point to are, on the one hand, that a sense of pragmatism rather than revolutionary idealism marked France's response to foreign revolutionaries, and she tended to support only those with potential for success; but on the other, that the element of bombastic rhetoric and freelancing which characterised every walk of French officialdom - especially less regulated areas like the secret service - fed the hopes of foreign revolutionaries and created the impression both in their own minds and in those of their home governments that French subversion was indeed a reality.

1. Early undercover activities in Britain, 1793-5.

The period from the outbreak of war between France and the continental monarchies in April 1792 and her declaration of war on Britain the following February witnessed an upsurge of heady internationalism in Paris culminating in the bombastic Edict of Fraternity of November 1792 with its promise of support to peoples wishing to liberate themselves. But even if the Irish, Scottish and English democrats who would subsequently organise revolutionary parties at home were deeply influenced by these republican festivities in Paris, before the Terror - and Robespierre in particular - revealed the inbred chauvinism of the new republic, France was unhappy about her developing image as the revolutionary mentor of Europe's dissidents. She was particularly anxious to appease neutral states such as England with

assurances that France had no intention of supporting every seditious
movement abroad:

> The Convention [wrote the French Foreign Minister
> Lebrun in December 1792] never intended to support every
> riot, to espouse the cause of every seditious movement,
> or to provoke disturbances in every neutral or friendly
> country; the idea is so below French dignity, that even
> to suggest it is to proffer a national insult. (4)

Even after the outbreak of war with England, France still harboured
almost sentimental feelings towards her as France's most natural ally (a
leftover from the early Enlightenment's Anglomania), failed to take up
quite definite requests for assistance from an Irish revolutionary
group, and confined most of her British intelligence activities to those
of information retrieval. But given the raw condition of France's
secret service after the Revolution and the royalist emigration, two
factors stand out in any study of early French revolutionary
intelligence: firstly, the constant use of interested foreign nationals,
for they were cheap at a time when the criteria applied to most
undercover operations was whether they were 'peu dispendieux' (5), with
the obvious disadvantage that they exaggerated French support and rarely
gave dispassionate reports; secondly, the lack of central control,
extending even to the absence of Foreign Ministry control over foreign
intelligence, which produced a bewildering proliferation of agents who
frequently spent more time spying on each other than on the enemy.

In the former context, France tended to use Irish agents for
England as well as Ireland – the main reason being that a genuine
conspiratorial movement did not emerge in England until 1797, and even
then remained confined to social groupings ill at ease in the world of
undercover diplomacy, which the largely professional, even aristocratic,
members of the United Irishmen moved in quite comfortably. Indeed when
the first purely English republican agents arrived on the continent
after British government purges in the spring of 1794 (the shoemaker and
former secretary of the London Corresponding Society, John Ashley, and
another prominent LCS member, Dr Robert Watson), they simply attached
themselves to the far more experienced groupings of United Irishmen in
Hamburg and Paris. True, there were a number of English radical
intellectuals in Paris in the early 1790s who were enthusiastic
supporters of France's revolution and war against the European
monarchies. But men such as the Society for Constitutional Information
members, John Hurford Stone and Sir Robert Smith (actually cashiered
from the British army for participating in the general renunciation of
all titles and honours at a republican celebration in Paris) and the
redoubtable Tom Paine himself, were far too well-known to the British
authorities to be of any use as intelligence agents. On the contrary,
the first secret agents sent to England after the outbreak of war were
ex-students of the Irish seminary in Paris, anonymous young men like
William Duckett, who led a mission composed of several fellow students
to England and Ireland which was to last until 1795. This early mission
was devoted largely to intelligence work rather than subversion (even if
Duckett took the initiative and joined the London Corresponding Society,
thereby establishing valuable links with the British democrats which he
would use to good effect later on). But France's continued use of
Duckett throughout the decade was an example of the more successful side

of the enforced necessity of using 'unknowns', and by 1797-8 when
Whitehall discovered his by now actively subversive role vis-à-vis the
British navy, ministers revealed their complete ignorance of his
activities, even to the extent of basic biographical details. Duckett
is an interesting character, for he symbolises the one main exception to
my claim that positive subversion was low on the list of instructions
issued to French agents in Britain in this period. From the outset
France did make positive efforts to undermine the loyalty of Britain's
armed forces, particularly the navy; Duckett was to become an
acknowledged expert in this field, and was widely suspected of having
been implicated in the Nore and Spithead mutinies of 1797.

Irish too was the ex-priest Nicholas Madgett, the officially-
sponsored organiser of a group of Anglo-Irish revolutionaries resident
in Paris in 1793, which functioned effectively as a pool of agents
servicing missions to the British Isles until 1796. It was an
unsatisfactory arrangement, for Madgett, as something of an empire-
builder, rarely resisted the temptation to embroider instructions;
certainly in the case of two extremely important missions for which he
acted as intermediary, those of the American Colonel Oswald to Ireland
in 1793 and of the Irish clergyman William Jackson to England and
Ireland in 1794-5, both agents were quite definitely offering more in
the way of positive French encouragement to foreign revolutionaries than
French governments of the day would have wished. Jackson would have
liked to have found a thriving democratic movement in England itself,
but his findings convinced him that there was none, and his elation at
discovering in Ireland such an advanced radical movement as the United
Irishmen was correspondingly all the greater. The English, he warned
France, 'are not friends of the French Revolution. And if they complain
somewhat, it is only because of the economic situation'. (6)   In
contrast he was deeply impressed by popular support for France in
Ireland, and the extension of his mission there was to result in his
arrest, trial and untimely death, when he committed suicide before a
startled Dublin courtroom. But this dramatic and public association of
the United Irishmen with foreign subversion confronted the society with
the choice of accepting the proffered French assistance and going
underground, or else of tamely agreeing to their own suppression. They
chose the former, and the upshot was the despatch to Paris of the young
Protestant barrister, Theobald Wolfe Tone, to negotiate for armed French
assistance. Jackson's mission is thus one of the many examples of
foreign radical groupings being pushed towards positive subversiveness
by interested freelancing – and is a salutary reminder that signs of
France's readiness to help those who rose against oppression were
frequently more apparent than real.

2. France's campaign of revenge against England, 1796-7.

The use of Irish agents for British missions became more pronounced
after Tone's establishment of an official United Irish mission in Paris
in 1796, necessitating frequent contact with both the home society and
later with its English offshoot, the United Englishmen. Native French
agents were still used, if infrequently so; but the example of one of
the longest information-gathering missions to England in these years, by
the Frenchman Jean Mengaud, shows clearly that positive subversion

44

(always excepting that involving Britain's armed forces) was not the general style of French undercover activities in England. Mengaud was despatched there in June 1796 with instructions to secure information on such topics as the state of British finances and (at a time when there was still some lingering French hope that the British were not entirely anti-French) on the attitudes of the British public and parliamentary opposition towards France. Mengaud soon laid such hopes to rest, decribing the British democrats as 'un petit troupeau isolé et sans pasteur' ('an isolated flock without a shepherd'), and pointing firmly to Ireland as the only part of the British Isles where France might assist a revolutionary movement with any chance of success. (7)

France had recently experienced a particularly rude awakening to the truth that the English were the new republic's worst enemy. For whilst France had not, on the whole, been guilty of the kind of subversive activities in England of which she was frequently accused (indeed Mengaud had actually been instructed to investigate reports that one of the French commissioners in London for the exchange of prisoners of war may have been guilty of such), Britain had fostered a particularly bloody civil war in France, financing royalist and federalist revolts and the infamous royalist expedition to Quiberon Bay in 1795. The Committee of Public Safety's statement about England having 'violated our national rights in a manner hitherto unknown', and of 'waging war ... by corruption rather than combat' (8) was not an example of political hypocrisy, but a token of the genuine sense of shock in France at the way in which England was conducting her war, and a new chauvinism and desire for revenge entered French war policy after these early experiences.

The arrival of Tone in Paris coincided with this temporary alteration in France's attitude towards England, and the desire to avenge the wrongs she had perpetuated on France became the driving force behind the actions of the two men most involved with the suppression of the war in the Vendée, General Hoche, the most respected military man in France before the meteoric rise of Bonaparte, and Lazare Carnot, one of the five-man Directory which governed France from 1795 to 1799. 'The aim of your mission will be to assist the establishment of a chouannerie (i.e. the type of banditry promoted by England in the west of France) in revenge for the atrocities committed daily by England on French territory', Carnot instructed a secret agent bound for England in June 1796, - the first mission of any significance there since the time of Jackson. (9) But if this mission to England by the young Bordeaux merchant, Jean Berthonneau, illustrates a very real desire in 1796 actively to promote subversion there, it is also illustrative of the tendency of political divisions in France to undermine such efforts. Carnot had sent Berthonneau to England independently of the French Foreign Ministry, which was under the control of a protégé of Reubell his political rival within the Directory, and the inefficiency and corruption of which he felt ill-attuned to the conduct of missions requiring the utmost secrecy. But the Foreign Minister discovered Carnot's subterfuge (not surprisingly, since the sheer extent of Berthonneau's task, involving plans to sabotage England's military arsenals, provoke food riots, prison riots, strikes, indeed everything to create internal havoc, would eventually have required Foreign

Ministry backing if only to secure communication through its existing network of agents), and attached his own agent to Berthonneau to report back and, it would appear, positively to sabotage this unorthodox mission. Indeed the choice of this second agent is indicative of the way in which espionage in the revolutionary period, as today, could take on a life of its own. Jean Colleville was an émigré, formerly in the employ of the royalist princes and now operating out of Hamburg as a double agent, with the knowledge of France, to which he was anxious to return without risking the normal penalties against those accused of emigration. It is hard to escape the conclusion, therefore, that his betrayal of Berthonneau's mission to the royalist agent in London, and through him to the British authorities, was done with full knowledge of the French Foreign Minister. As it was, poor Berthonneau was deserted on all sides once the truth was out and was in hiding, friendless and penniless, in Tottenham Court Road, London, when he was eventually recalled at the end of the year.

But the kind of freelancing, even at the highest political level, which this mission highlights, was typical of the conduct of France's secret service, making it difficult enough for the historian to ascertain the truth behind the scare stories of French subversion, let alone the foreign revolutionaries themselves, who were often the dupes of the inflated hopes thus generated. In 1796, such activities helped seal the fate of Carnot and his political supporters and militated against the fulfillment of such hopes by sparking off a reaction against practices which might justify the accusation, popular with France's enemies, that she fostered subversive activities everywhere. Certainly the news of the French-sponsored landing of convicts in Wales under General Tate in the spring of 1797 caused a public outcry in France. The 'ragamuffin' expedition, as it was dubbed at the time, was a spin-off from Berthonneau's chouannerie instructions and Hoche's attempted invasion of Ireland the previous December. But news of the landing broke upon a France in which the kind of unsavoury practices associated with Carnot's personal vendetta were no longer acceptable, and public reaction was to show just how misguided was the vision of French republicans as desperadoes bent on the destruction of established values and governments throughout Europe. French opinion generally favoured a military defeat of England rather than the kind of erosion of her internal strength envisaged by Carnot, and the hail of protest which greeted the Director's 1796 policy in the French legislative councils certainly showed that few wished to emulate England's example in the Vendée.

> I would like to know, [asked one deputy] ... if the
> executive Directory has the right to remove condemned
> men from the punishment which they have legally incurred
> .... Moreover, is this not a deeply immoral action which
> violates the rights of peoples ... and if our enemies
> are capable of such atrocities, must we imitate them or
> set the example? (10)

The failure of France's various efforts to weaken Britain in 1796 and early 1797 (notably the disastrous outcome of Hoche's major invasion attempt on Ireland) exacerbated the deteriorating relations between the legislature and the executive. Carnot's reputation was a particular casualty - he became increasingly isolated within the Directory and was finally removed in the coup d'état of Fructidor (September 1797).

3. British intelligence and the Nore and Spithead mutinies.

What I have suggested so far can scarcely justify the kind of scare mongering about subversive influence which Pitt's government used for instance, in the secret report of 1794, or in the justification of legislation such as the Alien Act, the Traiterous Correspondence Act of the same year, the 1794 Suspension of Habeas Corpus Act and the notorious 'Two Acts' (the Treason and Sedition Acts) of 1795. After all, these amounted to the suspension of the traditional rights of the 'freeborn Englishmen' which in popular parlance set England apart from the rest of Europe, and if Pitt's 'Terror' scarcely measured up to the Parisian one, it certainly did lead to the loss of freedom so valued in England in the eighteenth century. In the period up to 1797, however, British government fears were genuine enough and not simply an excuse for repressive legislation. The popular reform societies had not yet turned treasonable, but in the days before the Seditious Meetings Act of 1795, their mammoth meetings were disturbing, and were accompanied by increasingly bitter opposition from the parliamentary radicals. British intelligence emerged from the revolutionary wars in better shape than that of France, but however experienced a nation was in such matters, the French Revolution and the upsurge of dissident elements throughout Europe had created quite a novel situation. Intelligence professionals can only work according to patterns established through accrued experience of like situations. The situation presented to the established world by the upheavals of the 1790s was quite unusual, and it took time to adapt existing intelligence procedures. Not until 1797 did Britain secure the kind of inside information to indicate precisely what France and her disaffected subjects were up to, and by that date the alliance between the two had produced a movement which did justify government statements about domestic subversion, even if it did not about active French involvement. But before that information was tapped, the British government, still uncertain about the precise nature of French undercover activities on British territory, was confronted with an event which seemed to justify its worst fears: mutiny in the fleet.

The early years of the war had gone badly for England and in 1797 she faced France alone. Even her vaunted naval strength had failed to stop the major French invasion attempt on Ireland under General Hoche. Now her entire fleet was paralysed by a mutiny which many felt to be a delayed act of sabotage originally designed to coincide with Hoche's invasion attempt. The role of subversion in the Nore and Spithead mutinies has exercised the minds of historians for much of this century. The standard work, Dobrée and Mainwaring's Floating Republic dismisses such claims of French involvement, and there can be no doubt that the appalling conditions of service were the main cause of the outbreak. But recent research has revealed a definite attempt by France to seduce the loyalty of the sailors after the outbreak of war and the presence of a dangerously volatile element among the seamen which would have proved susceptible to such approaches. As regards the former, it is unlikely that the propaganda periodically circulated by France to British ships would have led to such a concerted outbreak; but a more determined

campaign was mounted by the French and their United allies to keep the
mutinies alive once they had started, and the volatile material was
there to work upon in the form of thousands of Irish rebels sent untried
into the navy under the stringent security legislation introduced to
cope with mounting discontent in Ireland. The prominence of such men in
the Nore mutiny in particular is beyond dispute, as are the attempts by
the United movement to keep it alive from onshore. Direct French
involvement is less clear, though as always France was happy enough for
republican allies to undertake this kind of sabotage and to be spared
both the expense and the taint of direct involvement. In all events,
there was enough evidence of subversion to justify Whitehall's fears
that year, even if excessive propaganda mileage was later derived from
it and the involvement of France in such activities was too erratic ever
to amount to any coherent undercover campaign on the British mainland.

4. Freelance intelligence and the emergence of the United Englishmen.

Despite this crescendo of subversive activity in 1796-7, the
political crisis in France and Bonaparte's victories in southern Europe
had altered the direction of France's war effort and transferred support
to the faction within the Directory which had always favoured the
concentration of military effort on the continent, rather than its
dispersal in unpredictable adventures overseas. And whilst the French
authorities were elated at this spectacle of England's prized navy
incapacitated by mutiny, there was no corresponding effort to capitalise
on this new development. The mutinies fed the Directors' complacency
about the strength of Irish sedition in the fleet and, much to Tone's
dismay, they did not share his sense of urgency that advantage should be
taken of the situation to send another force to Ireland.

Such complacency was not entirely unreasonable in view of the
developments in Britain's revolutionary underworld; for not only had the
French invasion attempt on Ireland produced a dramatic expansion of the
United Irish movement there, but on the mainland it had caused the more
moderate elements of the democratic societies to withdraw, leaving the
extreme radicals to join forces with the United Irishmen. The Directory
felt confident that the kind of pro-revolutionary movement it had sought
to create in Britain had finally emerged with the minimum of effort on
its part. Thereafter France quite happily left the task of subversion
in Britain to the dominant element in the new revolutionary alliance,
the United Irishmen, and Duckett was given a semi-permanent attachment
to the French legation in Hamburg to act as intermediary between the
Directory and the Irish agents. But Duckett's mission typifies the
continuing element of freelancing and lack of unanimity behind French
undercover activities. In the first place, the actions of Duckett, with
his own sense of mission and connections with the Irish and English
republicans, far exceeded those expected from the paid agent. Indeed
such were his continuing efforts to seduce the British sailors from
their loyalty that by 1798 his name had acquired considerable notoriety
in British intelligence channels. Secondly, it shows how the activities
of French attachés to foreign postings could sometimes lend France's
name to foreign subversion without official sanction, for Duckett's
attachment as private secretary to two official appointees in Hamburg
virtually turned the French offices there into outlets for the type of

subversive campaign which figured in Barruel's vision. Indeed, France's representatives abroad tended to be much more sympathetic towards foreign revolutionaries than the home government, to such an extent that the Directory felt obliged in 1798-9 to reprimand its officials for such lack of caution in the issue of passports to foreign patriots and to curtail the ease of access to France thus granted by these external channels. Lastly, it provides yet another example of the excessive individualism which so weakened the Directory, and the penchant for independent action by various departments was particularly pronounced in matters of secret service.

In the case of Duckett, he had remained intermittently in the service of his original employer, the Minister of the Marine, who despite frequent changes in personnel had a more consistent approach towards French-inspired subversion in Britain than the Foreign Ministry because of his department's obsession with Britain's so-called 'tyranny' of the seas (i.e. her undisputed naval supremacy). Moreover Bruix, the Marine Minister in 1797-8, had actually participated in Hoche's naval expedition to Ireland and had introduced a note of pro-revolutionary zeal unrepresentative of post-Fructidorean policies. Thus when Ireland finally rebelled in 1798, he sent Duckett on another secret mission, this time to take substantial financial aid (28,000 livres – over £1,000). Given the absence of the bulk of her army and her best generals in Egypt with Bonaparte, the efforts of France to get military aid to the Irish rebels were impressive. The changing attitudes towards internal British subversion after 1796-7 did not necessarily mean a total abandonment of foreign republicans; rather, it represented an extension of Robespierre's pragmatic approach, with the French helping those who helped themselves – and France proved as good as her word when the Irish eventually did rebel. But the persistence of this practical military outlook towards internal British disaffection, even at the height of the heady internationalism of 1792-3, shows that direct French subversion was never as systematic nor as insidious as scaremongers in British officialdom claimed – certainly under Napoleon even French republicanism, let alone the foreign variety, was frowned upon. Former republicans were an embarrassment to Bonaparte in his quest for respectability and he tended to favour military rather than undercover campaigns against his enemies.

In terms of indirect subversion, however, the success of France is undeniable. Expectations of French help sustained a formidable revolutionary underground in Ireland, whose strength in the field came as a shock to England in the 1798 rebellion, and though the mainland movement was paltry in comparison, its main aim was a diversionary one, to detract the troops from the main attempt in Ireland, and its campaign to subvert the loyalty of Britain's armed forces caused considerable concern in London.

5. The machinery of subversion: spies and subsidies.

A final estimate of French subversion in Britain must also take into account the machinery of subversion, notably through the spy and intelligence network. Spies and secret agents, though such a necessary instrument of war administration, were publicly frowned upon in England

and France alike. The British and French archives abound with their
scribbled reports and often exaggerated statements. But if both
countries treated them with a healthy scepticism, England actually
incorporated such scepticism into her organisation of what became an
increasingly effective and professional espionage network by the late
1790s. For, by working on the assumption that salaried spies would not
be tempted to tailor their information to secure better rewards, Britain
dispensed with the casually-paid spy and made espionage a reliable
profession for the trusted few.

In contrast, French agents, after the example of Oswald in 1793,
were not paid in advance, and though under the Directory they were given
an initial lump sum to defray immediate travel costs, further payment
was only made on the basis of information delivered, and their expenses
claims were closely scrutinised and rarely fully met. For example,
Duckett's immediate employer in Hamburg, the ex-Jacobin Léonard Bourdon,
acting there as a kind of eighteenth-century spy-master, was allocated
19,370 livresfor his eight-month mission (approximately £810) In itself
this was quite generous by French standards (the resident French
minister to the Hanseatic towns received an annual payment of 30,000
livres), and one might live quite comfortably for seven shillings a day.
However of that sum, Bourdon was paid only 4,000 on his departure from
France, a further 1,200 livres was sent by the Foreign Minister in the
course of his mission, 5,600 paid out on his return, and he was still
petitioning for the remainder in December 1800, over two years after the
termination of his mission. And yet this mission, involving
instructions to penetrate the émigré underworld in northern Europe and
to act as intermediary between Paris and secret agents to Britain, was
clearly intended to be the focus of the most extensive undercover
campaign against Britain since the opening of the war. But it was also
the product of a temporary Jacobin resurgence in France and fell victim,
like so many other missions before it, to a change of political
temperature in Paris.

Some French politicians were clearly averse to extensive undercover
activities, preferring to concentrate financial resources on the
military campaign against France's enemies. Indeed the Foreign
Minister, sending returns of only 200,000 livres (£8,100) on foreign
secret expenditure for the year 1799-1800, boasted it as a token of the
new republic's purity in contrast to the enormous secret budgets of the
old monarchies, and remarked with some satisfaction on the example to
Europe of 'the restriction which the republican government imposes upon
itself in such matters. It [Europe] would be more peaceful if the
British government acted with the same reserve'. (11) Certainly the
subsidies sent by Britain to the counter-revolution in France were
staggering (£ 10,000 spent on the attempt to influence one set of
elections in France alone, with the agents authorised to draw on a
further £ 50,000 if necessary). (12) But the Foreign Minister's figures
are somewhat debatable, disguising as they do large quantities paid out
in paper money, in assignats or in mandats, and overall one suspects
that he was making a virtue of necessity. For the main reason for such
parsimony was the national bankruptcy which had persisted since before
the revolution and which the sale of confiscated church and noble
property had done little to alleviate. Financial wastage of any

description was considered unforgiveable, and the type of circular so common in the 1970s, urging economy in the use of lighting and stationery, was familiar to every clerk in French government employ. Under the Directory sufficient money was never forthcoming for naval expeditions, let alone such minor items as secret service expenditure. Little wonder that ministers fought bitterly over who was responsible for paying returned agents, or that they should have preferred to use United Irish agents, for the costs of the latter were often paid by the home organisation and their commitment to the weakening of British power seemed guaranteed to produce results.

The erratic nature of France's secret service is also reflected in the multiplicity of sources for information about intelligence during the revolutionary period. Secret service payments in England were made only by the Secretaries of State for the Home and Foreign Offices and by the First Lord of the Admiralty, and from 1794 the control of the foreign secret service was totally vested in the Foreign Secretary. The personnel involved in organising British espionage remained virtually unchanged throughout this period and a similar continuity of personnel can be detected among the agents themselves. In France, however, foreign secret service money was confined to no one minister and for the first year of the war officials were not accountable for their expenditure in this field. Consequently sources are scattered through the papers of the Marine, Foreign and War Ministries, the Police bureau and a multitude of other officials who had power to divert money from the national treasury for such purposes. Procedure for secret service expenditure was gradually rationalised under the Directory and by 1796 the Foreign Minister was officially responsible for organising the foreign intelligence service. In practice, however, the chaotic procedure of previous years persisted, for the Directors preferred to operate through a minister of their own political hue if the Foreign Minister happened to be a supporter of their rivals. The main example of this process was the tendency of successive Marine Ministers to dabble in undercover missions to England in particular (because of their continuing crusade against British naval supremacy), and overall the missions sponsored by this Ministry tended to be much more subversive than those arising in Foreign Affairs. On paper the danger of conflicting missions had been solved with the removal of responsibility for commercial and consular postings abroad from the Marine Minister in February 1793. In practice the overlap continued.

Another pointer to the French Republic's rawness in these matters is reflected in the kind of documentary evidence confronting the researcher. I am thinking in particular of the contrast between the carefully decoded letters from foreign agents in the British Foreign Office papers and the boxes of charred and brittle letters in the French equivalent. Many French agents still used the unsatisfactory secret ink method which was brought out by exposure to a naked flame; and after weeks of attempting to read Berthonneau's blackened letters through a powerful magnifying glass, I fully sympathised with the French Foreign Minister's exasperated comment that they were 'presqu'illisible'!

However, to look to the admittedly chaotic nature of French espionnage in this period and to conclude that the fear of French subversion was mere panic-mongering would be a gross simplification. Groundless propaganda was not Britain's style, even if the careful juxtaposition of facts in the various secret committee reports of the 1790s was designed to magnify the threat. Whilst indiscriminate revolutionary activity abroad was never common French practice, moral encouragement, backed up with some military aid if they proved themselves in a rising, was normally extended to the disaffected of enemy countries - and moral encouragement alone, turning Paris into a magnet for foreign revolutionaries throughout Europe, is not to be dismissed as a factor in the fostering of subversive movements abroad. In the case of Britain, France was prepared to go much further. Her involvement in the Vendée, the fact that she was the main force in the coalition against France, and for much of the period the only remaining combattant, caused the Directory to negotiate seriously with Britain's internal dissidents in a way which it was clearly unwilling to do in the case of many other foreign revolutionaries. Such encouragement was to change the United Irishmen from an advanced reform movement into a militantly republican one by 1796, to cause it to set up official undercover missions in Paris and London, and in England to attach the scattered recesses of mainland conspiracy to its extended campaign to win Irish independence and topple the British government, if not the monarchy itself. In the period 1796-8 France despatched five naval expeditions to Ireland and incalculable quantities of arms, and whilst already disabused of the idea of rebellion on the English mainland, France still hoped that a successful campaign in Ireland would provide a back door to England herself, with the pockets of revolution organised in the United Englishmen conducting simultaneous acts of sabotage. Nor was this vision totally unrealistic, and with the blunders and naval mistakes of England herself prior to 1797 it is hard not to conclude that only an incredible series of accidents saved her from the implementation of this plan at the time of Hoche's attempt in 1796. That a French protectorate in Ireland would necessarily have brought about a similar development in England is highly doubtful - but France's main war aim in sponsoring the United movement was to push England out of the war, and given the existence of a strong peace movement in England, particularly among the parliamentary opposition, it seems highly likely that the added threat in Ireland may well have forced England to make peace. Subversion for England and France alike was merely another weapon in the war, a preliminary to a military offensive, rand in this respect Barruel's comment on French tactics is quite correct:

> ... its plots, its legions of secret agents, its propaganda are sent everywhere as a precursor to its armies .... It wins public opinion before it sends in its Pichegru or Bonaparte, its traitors created to open the frontier gates ....' (12)

The relative success of French subversion abroad can therefore only fully be calculated in terms of its military outcome and in this sense its British campaign must be reckoned a failure. But the United movement was much stronger than anything created in Holland or Italy before the French armies moved in, and we can safely conclude that it was Britain's superior naval strength that prevented her from military defeat at the height of French confidence in 1796 rather than the failure of the latter's efforts to weaken her internally.

Notes

1. Report from the Committee of Secrecy of the House of Commons relative to the proceedings of different persons and societies in Great Britain and Ireland engaged in a treasonable conspiracy (London, 1799), and Report from the Committee of Secrecy of the House of Commons on the State of Ireland (London, 1801).

2. G. A. Williams, Artisans and Sans Culottes, (London, 1968), pp. 74 and 80.

3. 'Conspiracy or Anti-Conspiracy - propaganda and the revolutionary threat in late eighteenth-century England', unpublished paper delivered at the Institute of Historical Research, London.

4. Archives des Affaires Etrangères, Paris, Corr. Pol. Ang. 584. fos. 177-8.

5. Archives Nationales, AF II* 2 fos. 247-8.

6. Archives des Affaires Etrangères, Corr. Pol. Ang. 588 fos. 168-9.

7. Ibid., 591 fos. 174-188.

8. Ibid., 588 fos. 47-50.

9. Archives historiques de la Guerre, Vincennes, Paris, BB[11] 1.

10. Archives Nationales, AF III 437 doss. 2527 fo. 43.

11. Archives Nationales, AF III 52-5 doss. 213 plaq. 4 fo. 65

12. See W. R. Fryer, Republic or Restoration in France? 1794-97, (Manchester, 1965) pp. 196-7.

British Counter-revolutionary Popular Propaganda in the 1790's

ROBERT HOLE

The masterpiece of counter-revolutionary propaganda Burke's Reflections on the Revolution in France, was published in early November 1790. Like all his later pieces on the same theme, it was designed for an educated readership well versed in history and philosophy, and provided an intellectual critique of the Revolution and defence of the traditional British social and political system. That system depended for its security not only on law and coercion but also upon customary acceptance by the bulk of the nation. The traditional patterns of social control had already been somewhat disrupted by economic changes; now, as Burke was acutely aware, they were being challenged directly. It was clear that if the lower orders were to be kept in a position of social subordination, the revolutionary ideology had to be confronted at a popular level. However, although Burke recognised the need, he left the execution of the task to other pens. How these writers of popular propaganda countered the threat which the French Revolution posed to the established order in Britain, and how directly they drew on Burke's inspiration, is the subject of this article.

1. The major phases of counter-revolutionary pamphleteering in the 1790s

In the early years of the Revolution, and indeed throughout the 1790s, much, perhaps most, propaganda in Britain took an oral form. Hannah More, who had abandoned her life as an eminent blue-stocking in fashionable society to devote herself to religion and good works, turned seriously to pamphlet writing only in the second half of the decade. Between 1789 and 1795 she produced only one pamphlet (Village Politics in 1792), most of her time was devoted to the foundation of schools for the poor which taught religious principles, political loyalty and social subordination. Before the autumn of 1792 only a few genuinely popular counter-revolutionary tracts were produced in Britain. One such was the pseudonymous John Nott's Very Familiar Letters, addressed to Dr. Priestley (1790), but this crude and abusive pamphlet could have had little meaning beyond the Birmingham audience for which it was designed. Otherwise, a few established writers addressed themselves to the labouring population but, like William Paley, the Archdeacon of Carlisle, in his Reasons for Contentment (1792), they did so in a form and language inaccessible to most.

THE CONTRAST

1793

BRITISH LIBERTY

FRENCH LIBERTY

RELIGION.   MORALITY.   ATHEISM,   PERJURY
LOYALTY, OBEDIENCE to the LAWS,   REBELION.TREASON.ANARCHY.MURDER.
INDEPENDANCE, PERSONAL SECURITY,   EQUALITY,MADNESS,CRUELTY,INJUSTICE.
JUSTICE, INHERITANC, PROTECTION of   TREACHERY, INGRATITUDE, IDLENESS.
PROPERTY,INDUSTRY,NATIONAL PROSPERITY   FAMINE,NATIONAL&PRIVATE RUIN.
HAPPINESS.   WHICH IS BEST?   MISERY.

All this was transformed in late 1792. From November 1792 to January 1793 a flood of counter-revolutionary pamphlets appeared. To a considerable extent this was the result of the activities of the 'Association for Preserving Liberty and Property against Republicans and Levellers'. The Association, which held its meetings at the Crown and Anchor in the Strand, was established by John Reeves in November 1792. It sought to rally conservative opinion against the growing number of radical societies. While independent of government, it had the support and encouragment of the administration and led to the formation of a large number of loyalist associations throughout the country. The Crown and Anchor Association made a major effort to meet the rising tide of radical propaganda with its own publications. These took two forms. Firstly a number of serious and fairly intelligent pamphlets were printed by direct order of the Association. These included John Bowles's A Protest against T.Paine's 'Rights of Man' (1792) and Archdeacon Paley's Reasons for Contentment (1792) both of which had been published before but which now reached a much wider audience. Secondly the Association sponsored the publication of a number of popular tracts for the lower classes. These were chosen and approved not by the committee itself but by 'a person in whom they confided'. About fifty of these penny tracts were issued in November and December 1792 and republished in collected form in January 1793. In addition to these, a considerable number of other counter-revolutionary popular tracts were published independently of the Association during the same three months. While fundamentally the same, these tend on the whole to be cruder and more scurrilous than those produced by the Association.

Both the formation of the Association and the outpouring of tracts were a response to recent events in France and England. In France the Revolution appeared to be taking a more radical and a more violent turn with the September Massacres (2nd-3rd September), the abolition of the monarchy (21st September) and the trial of the King (11th December-18th January) leading to his execution on 21st January 1793. French military victories at Valmy in September and Jemappes in November suggested that the Revolution could spread to other countries and this threat was reinforced by the Convention's Edict of Fraternity of 19th of November 1792 promising 'assistance to all people who wished to recover their liberty', although the tracts make surprisngly few references to this decree. In England meanwhile, Thomas Paine's Rights of Man, the second part of which had been published in February 1792, was being distributed widely. This distribution was, in part organised by the large number of radical societies whose membership grew significantly in the ensuing months. By the end of the year the Government was taking reports of possible insurrection seriously and considered the London Corresponding Society a real danger. In November the Sheffield Constitutional Society celebrated the French military victories publically. Congratulatory addresses were sent to the Convention in Paris from a number of radical societies, with London and Scotland going so far as to dispatch fraternal delegations. The effects of radical activity amongst the poor, encouraging discontent, were exacerbated by the problems of food shortages, high prices and low wages, and unrest was widespread with riots in Scotland and North East England. Many were ready to believe allegations of a radical plot to seize London in early December. These circumstances in France and in England combined to create widespread fear and a crisis of confidence amongst the British establishment in the autumn and winter of 1792-1793. The propaganda pamphlets were designed significantly to alter the climate of public opinion and to prepare the British people for a possible war against the French.

These publications of late 1792 and early 1793 represent the most intense phase of the ideological pamphlet war. Doubtless many of them continued to be circulated and reissued in the following months and even years. Certainly the production of counter-revolutionary popular propaganda continued throughout the rest of the decade and many of the same arguments were used but never in so concentrated, political and urgent a form. It was as if the moment of crisis had been passed. Later pamphlets could afford to be more selective in their aim, more relaxed in their argument. They supported the war against France strongly; any suggestion of a premature peace before Jacobinism was destroyed and the monarchy restored was firmly resisted. The people needed to be strengthened in their resolve during the scarcity of 1795 and in the dark days of 1797 when the naval mutinies were denounced and hope and faith in eventual victory reaffirmed.

The world of the popular pamphlet in the second half of the decade was, however, dominated by Hannah More and the Cheap Repository Tracts. These were published from 1795 to 1798 at the rate of about three a month; by 1798 nearly two million had been sold at a halfpenny or a penny each. They were circulated in workplaces, schools, hospitals, prisons and workhouses, in the army and navy and through booksellers, hawkers and fair ground stallholders. Nearly half of them were written by Hannah More herself, and all of them had to meet with her approval. They are a world apart from the 1792-93 tracts. The frantic political assertions of those years are replaced by the expression of timeless spiritual values; political expediency is transformed into moral crusade.

To what extent do the popular pamphlets of the 1790s reflect Burke's thinking? In a superficial sense it is possible to argue that their content was dictated more by Paine than Burke, the agenda of debate set more by Rights of Man than by the Reflections. Generally speaking, as we shall see, Burke influenced not so much the arguments of the tracts as their attitudes and assumptions. Certainly these pamphlets are far more (and less) than simply a translation of the Reflections into popular language. It would be a mistake to cast an analysis of them in purely Burkean terms. To understand the precise nature of Burke's indirect and somewhat limited influence, it is necessary first to examine the arguments of the tracts independently. Moreover this examination needs to be set in the context of their overall method and approach. Propaganda and ideology employ many more techniques than mere straightforward argument. They seek to structure a specific vision of reality which depends more upon perception than understanding and the arguments they employ are to some extent influenced by those wider propaganda techniques. This article will concentrate largely upon the political pamphlets of 1792-93 and on the Cheap Repository Tracts of 1795-98 which represent the two major strands of counter-revolutionary popular propaganda in the decade. Only after analysing the arguments of these two groups of tracts in the context of their own propaganda methods will it be possible to assess Burke's influence upon them.

2. The pamphlets of 1792-93: range and styles

The popular pamphlets, broadsheets and ballads of 1792-93 were addressed generally to the industrious poor and specifically to a range of occupations in the lower and lower middle orders of society: merchants, tenant farmers, craftsmen, tradesmen, shopkeepers, publicans, servants, mechanics, artificers, manufacturers and labourers. While the arguments they present are fundamentally the same, the tracts range considerably in their style, their intellectual level and their form.

The style of presentation is varied to suit the particular group for whom the tract was written. Theodore Price, for example, writing under the pseudonym of 'Job Nott, Bucklemaker, of Birmingham' aimed at a fairly low level urban audience. Job Nott's Humble Advice appeared in early December 1792 and was followed on the first day of the new year by The Life and Adventures of Job Nott which reached an eleventh edition by 1798. Posing as a 'brother artificer' he sought credibility by the inclusion of coarse and explicit scatological jokes at the expense of the Paineites and enlivened his arguments with amusing escapades which have only limited polemical purpose. But although the jam is distinctive, the pill is conventional. The Birmingham flavour is quite strong with much emphasis being placed on the role of the Dissenters and upon manufacturing interests, but the arguments and moral attitudes remain the same as in the other tracts written for a rural audience or for a specific occupation. He praises the Sunday Schools and supports education for the poor, though he refuses to learn French, wanting nothing to do "with such a nation, while ruled by such bloody minded barbarians, why they are worse than the Antipoads that kill'd and chop'd our brave sailor Captain Cook to pieces."

Different tracts also aimed at a variety of intellectual levels within the popular market. This is illustrated by the series of Bull family letters written by William Jones, the religious controversialist. One Pennyworth of Truth (1792), a letter from Thomas Bull to his brother John, together with John's two relies, aim towards the lower part of the range. They are vigorous but contain little argument and cover only a narrow field. They do not, however, plumb the depths of One Pennyworth More (1792), Thomas's second letter to John. This broadsheet was issued on 12th December and unlike most of the Bull letters was not published by the Association. It ranks amongst the crudest and lowest of all the tracts of this period and tells how the French "picked two famous Englishmen, Thomas Paine and the Birmingham Doctor to... assist them in the Work of teaching John Bull to eat Revolution Soup, dished up with human-flesh and French Pot-Herbs. I love liberty with Law such as we have in England, as well as anybody does; but that Liberty without Law, which makes men eat one another, can only come from the devil who would eat us all." By contrast A Letter from John Bull to his Countrymen (1792), while still popular in tone, includes a range of well presented arguments, and Thomas's letter to his second cousin John Bull Esquire,

58

of 30th January 1793, lifts the case onto a much higher intellectual plane and indeed can hardly be considered popular at all.

The lower the intellectual level becomes, the more the tracts depend upon various emotional devices rather than argument. The use of the kind of stereotypes popularised in visual form in the cartoons of Gillray and others was very common. "The numerous family of the Bulls (who have been admired by foreigners for their fat, jolly, rosy faces and round bellies)" is archetypal. They eat roast beef and plum puddings and are "blunt, honest, sensible." John Bull claims "honesty signifies fidelity, perseverance, and integrity. I possess them ALL". The other tract writers claimed to be simple, honest and industrious. Frenchmen, by comparison have "thin jaws and lank guts", the result of their diet of "French frogs and soup meagre:. They are "saucy and envious, unreliable and deceitful.(1) The only Englishmen who would become Jacobins are the idle and propertyless beggars, drunkards, cheats, vagabonds and thieves. Revolutionary principles are equated with French influences, and traditional patriotic and xenophobic sentiments are exploited and harnessed to the counter-revolutionary cause.

The choice of names assists the simple readers in distinguishing the reliable from the subversive - David Trusty, Thomas Steady, Sir John Blunt, Justice Worthy... and Judas MacSerpent! Proverbial wisdom is frequently invoked: the Englishmen's house is his castle, Paineites are wolves in sheep's clothing, and by their faults shall Jacobins be known. Traditional stories are employed: the poor are warned against killing the goose that lays the golden eggs: AEsop's fable of the sheep who, incited by wolves, revolt from the government of the dogs only to be eaten, is frequently recounted, and his story about the need for co-operation between head, feet and heart if the body is to function is used as an allegory of the organic state. Traditional folk wisdom is made to appear anti-revolutionary in many tracts, but especially in those lowest in the intellectual range.

The forms which published propaganda took also varies a great deal. Considerable use was made both of cartoons and ballads. The Association recognised the value and powerful impact of cartoons and commissioned a number of them. Like the tracts, the cartoons varied in their intellectual levels. Gillray's work was often subtler, ironic and equivocal; many other cartoonists were crude, direct and obvious. One of the prints most widely circulated amongst the lower orders was The Contrast (? Rowlandson, after Lord George Murray) which presents in graphic form a constant theme of the tracts. It was published in January 1793 and sold for only threepence. It was also used as the frontispiece of The Antigallican Songster (1793) one of a number of collections of popular ballads published at this time. The Association, aware of the need 'to serve all tastes' sponsored, the printing of a number of what one of its critics admitted were 'very delectable ballads'.(2) They were designed to be sung to various well known tunes such as 'Hearts of Oak' or 'O The Golden Days of Good Queen Bess'. They catered for the popular end of the market and often summarised in simple form the arguments and stories of the longer pamphlets.

These longer tracts also vary in their form. Some are direct and

vigorous polemics, others heavy-handed satirical spoofs. A few purport
to be republications of extracts from French papers and pamphlets and
are designed to discredit the Revolution. But the most common form is
the dialogue. John Bowles attempted to present the arguments of his
Protest against T.Paine's 'Rights of Man'(1792) in three Dialogues on
the Rights of Britons between a Farmer, a Sailor and a Manufacturer
(1792), but a truly popular style eluded him. Hannah More struck a more
convincing note in Village Politics (1792), a brilliant precis of almost
all the major arguments, compressed crisply and precisely into five
thousand words of dialogue between Jack Anvil the blacksmith and Tom Hod
the mason. Look before ye Loup (1793) provided a Scottish version but it
is only the language which is translated, the arguments are identical.
Almost all the dialogues follow a similar form. A well-intentioned but
credulous fellow has met Paineites in the local inn, been seduced by
their subversive ideas and given a copy of Rights of Man which has
destroyed his previous contentment. He discusses these ideas, which he
only half understands, with either a friend of the same class or a
sympathetic social superior who explains kindly why all these arguments
are invalid. The dialogue invariably ends with the misguided man seeing
the error of his ways and reaffirming his loyalty to King and Constitution.

3. The pamphlets of 1792-93: ideas and arguments

Despite the great variety of style, intellectual level and form in
these pamphlets of 1792-93, certain arguments and propaganda techniques
are constant. Radical ideas are challenged both on empirical and
normative grounds. One level of empirical argument is highly specific,
namely those parts of the tracts which attempt to counter Paine's
detailed allegations regarding the monarchy, taxes and the electoral
system. Only a few feel it is necessary to vindicate the hereditary
principle, but most defend the royal income. Conceding that the King
receives a million pounds a year, they anxiously explain that from it he
pays the ministers, the judges and many other useful and necessary
officers. They concede that taxes are high, but insist that they are
essential: the fleet and the army has to be paid for and the American
War (which was largely caused, they suggest, by Paine's agitation) has
resulted in a large national debt which must be paid off. Anyway, if
taxes were reduced or tithes abolished, the poor would be no better off
for wages would fall and rents rise. Taxation in Britain is fair, they
explain, for the rich, far from being exempt, pay more than the poor.
The present system of unequal representation in Parliament is defended;
the men elected are virtuous and represent all the nation fairly. One
tract, A Few Plain Questions and a little Honest Advice to the Working
People of Great Britain (1792), suggests moreover that Leeds, Manchester, Birmingham and Sheffield are prosperous because they have not
had election campaigns to distract men from their work. Behind all this
specious justification, lies the very real fear of the propertied
classes that reform would let the mob in. The Englishman's Catechism
(1792) warned small property-owners
if the mode of election be altered, and the
scale of it extended, men of property, in-

terested by that property in the real welfare
and stability of the nation, would not be
chosen; but cunning, low-minded men who had
nothing to lose. Actuated by the lust of power
and gain, under the mask of Equality, they
would give the watchword to their friends
without doors - declare the King and Lords
useless (as the case was in the days of Cromwell), and fabricate what they would call a
Republic, but, in other words, a violent
userpation of all the lands and property of
the kingdom, which would be at the disposal of
them and their adherents.
The passing reference to Cromwell in this passage is fairly rare in
these tracts. Generally they did not assume their readers knew any
history. The term 'levellers' to describe those who would abolish
distinctions in society is very commonly used but almost always in a
purely contemporary sense which suggests that no reference to the
seventeenth century group was intended.

On a more general level of empirical argument, the tracts seek to
challenge the Paineite accounts both of France and of Britain and to
present instead 'true' pictures. In France, they claim, the Revolution
has inflicted great hardship upon the poor. Because productive work has
stopped there are shortages and starvation. Repeatedly the tracts tell
of how the French have been forced to make a paste of bran and cabbage
leaves in place of bread. The more extreme relate how a starving mother
ate her baby. The French army is depicted as not only starving but
marching without shoes or proper uniforms; Job Nott alleges the soldiers were sent into cold countries "to fight up to their backsides in
snow with no breeches". The September Massacres and their aftermath in
Paris and the provinces are fully exploited to demonstrate the horror of
revolution. Thomas Bull assured his readers he knew eye-witnesses from
his own country who had been in Paris and seen priests massacred and had
watched the blood of the victims run from the mouths of their murderers.
Job Nott imaginatively invokes Burke's name to add credibility to a
similar tale when he refers to "the French Cannibals (as Mr Burke justly
called 'em for he said they cut out Gentlemen's hearts, and squeezed the
blood into wine and drank it.(3) Burke had, of course, said nothing of
the kind; this is merely one of a number of tales of horror and violence
which were frequently repeated in vivid and gory detail.

Just as in the cartoons, so in the tracts this picture of France is
contrasted to an ideal vision of Britain. She is depicted as the most
prosperous country on earth, with extensive trade and commerce, the envy
of the world. The living standard of the vast majority of the population
is steadily improving; one eighty-year-old father looks at his son's
white bread, tea and sugar and his cotton clothes and reflects how much
better things are now than in his youth.(4) How can one conceive of
changing a system which works so well? The rich benefit society by their
charity, providing hospitals, infirmaries, dispensaries and free
schools. The orphaned, old and infirm are provided for out of the Poor
Rate. And for the able-bodied, there is in Britain the opportunity for
self-improvement, if only a person is sufficiently industrious. Wealth

and prosperity are not restricted to a closed caste, they are open to all willing to work to achieve them - the proof is provided by a large cast of characters in the tracts who have themselves made good.The real distinction in society, the tracts imply, is not between the rich and the poor, as the French revolutionaries are thought to claim, but rather between the idle and the industrious.

The counter-revolutionary tracts thus offer a highly ideological presentation of supposed empirical facts. Besides this, they also confront their opponents normative arguments. Their tactic here, however, is first to misrepresent and distort them out of all recognition. This is seen very clearly in their attack on the concept of equality, which is seen as crucial to the Jacobin's arguments and which is therefore a major target for attack by the pamphleteers. Although they purport to challenge Paine's ideas, in fact the tracts address themselves not to his modest and cautious position but to one carried to the mathematical extreme. If all the money in the country were divided equally everyone would have an income of about one hundred and fifty pounds per annum, so all could live like gentlemen - but who then would produce the goods necessary to life, who would plough, grind corn and bake? If all the land in the country were divided equally everyone could have three acres each - but if all were equal husbandmen how could the economy function without the necessary specialist crafts? Moreover, the removal of the rich from the economy would destroy the market for luxury goods and thus cause unemployment among their manufacturers. Even if a state of precise mathematical equality were established it would last only briefly for, as John Bull's Second Answer to his Brother Thomas (1792) suggests, "the honest, sober, industrious, saving man will increase his property; while the lazy, sculking, drunken rascal, will remain poor and miserable". So, besides the economic arguments, the tracts assert man's natural inequality. Some men are evidently stronger, more enterprising, more intelligent than others. It is self-evident that women are not equal to men nor children to adults. Finally, the commonsense economics and the claims that inequality is natural are buttressed by religious arguments. Inequality is decreed not by man but by divine Providence; to challenge it is to flout the will of God.

The tracts then use this extreme and ridiculous form of equality (which they have themselves invented) to discredit the Paineite conception of the Rights of Man. They contrast these spurious rights with the 'real' rights of men, embodied in the established order in Britain and safe-guarded by the existence of laws which apply to all. The laws of Britain, they claim, defend men's natural rights by protecting life and limb, their religious rights by establishing toleration, and their civil rights by securing their property and allowing freedom of movement and action, only excepting those acts of wickedness, immorality or injustice which would infringe the rights of others. True liberty, they argue, is to be found not in equality but in security - of life and property. "I have property" declares a small farmer, "and I do not choose to live where the first beggar I meet may, the sabre in one hand, and the Rights of Man in the other, demand a share of that which a good government tells me is my own."(5) Men have, by their labour or that of their ancestors, established a right to their property, whether it is a rich man's castle, a poor man's cottage, a servant's wages or a carpenter's chest of tools. In Britain the tracts claim, rich and poor stand equal before the law, secure in the possession of their goods. No one reading these tracts would guess that the French Declaration of the Rights of Man which Paine translated and discusses in his book affirms that men are "equal in respect of their rights... and these rights are liberty, property, security, and resistance of oppression"!

The way in which these arguments are developed contributes towards the major propaganda technique of these pamphlets - the engendering of unity through fear. They seek to persuade the lower middle classes and the industrious poor that any property they possess, however little, would be threatened if the Jacobins, either the English or the French variety, gained control in Britain. They impute dishonest motives to their opponents. 'Tam Thrum, an auld weaver' of Edinburgh asserts in Look before ye Loup (1793) that the radical "ringleaders are making stepping-stones of the common fo'k, an' they'll kick them awa as soon as they have ser'd their ends". 'Strap Bootkin, staymaker' warns in his Address to the Members of the Various Box Clubs and Benefit Societies in Great Britain (1792) that Paineites are infiltrating well-established friendly societies and using the money originally collected to support the old and sick, for political purposes and their own personal ends. Paine is consistently denigrated, especially in the ballads. He and the English Jacobins are depicted as being in French pay. They are idle men who, being unwilling to acquire property through their own industry, seek to seize it in the general disruption following social and political upheaval. This is why it is unsafe to reform Parliament: "it is not prudent to open the door to carpenters and masons for the repair of a building, when a set of lawless ruffians are ready to rush in, totally to destroy the edifice, for the sake of what they can plunder." (6) However little you possess, whether it is a single guinea's worth of furniture, a shilling in your pocket, a spare shirt or a pair of stockings which could be stolen, you are at risk and your interest is one with those who would defend property.

> If a duke or an earl has not a right to his great estate, what right has the small landowner to his freehold? - What right has the shopkeeper to his shop, the tenant to his farm, the corporation to its privileges and freedom, the master tradesman to the work of his apprentices and servants, or any working man to his comfortable meal, while there is a beggar in the street that wants it? All and each of these rights depend on the established law of the land, protecting property as it happens to stand: Destroy it as to the great properties, and the small will not be long following.(7)

This, perhaps, is counter-revolutionary ideology at its most reactionary. At a time when class consciousness was beginning to emerge, when the working class were becoming aware they had a specific economic interest distinct from that of the governing class in Britain, the tracts reaffirm the old-fashioned notion of a whole community united in a common interest.

The central arguments of the late 1792-early 1793 tracts are
immediate, practical and secular. To adapt one of Job Nott's metaphors,
the dyke was leaking and had urgently to be plugged with any and every
material to hand. At this time, the more reflective, spiritual arguments
were somewhat overshadowed by the direct political and economic polemics, but they were not entirely absent. The tracts reminded their
readers that true happiness is to be found in a contented mind. The poor
man with a healthy diet, bread, cheese and English beer, has a sound
appetite and digestion and sleeps easily. The rich man, burdened with
worries about his complex business, his health ruined by fine food and
excessive drink, can rarely sleep more than two hours at a stretch.
Religious faith offered the poor comforts in the deprivations of this
life, hope of joy in the world to come, and a threat of eternal punishment. The tracts see Christianity as a bulwark against revolution. They
point out that atheism preceded revolution in France for, as a French
Jacobin explained in the dialogue The Plot Found Out (1792), "we cannot
bring people to our purposes if they fear God and Honour the King:. In
England many determine not to "run the hazard of eternal misery".(8)
Some writers make greater appeals to religion than others. Thomas Bull
relies heavily upon it in his defence of monarchy while John Bowles
makes no reference to it at all. Most writers at this time seem to use
it as a final safetynet to catch those few remaining hearts missed by
the more immediate arguments. Even Hannah More makes only passing
reference to it in Village Politics (1792). She spells out the ob-
ligations imposed on christians to submit to government quoting the
three traditional texts, Luke XX 25, Romans XIII 1, and I Peter II 17 -
"Render to Caesar...", "the powers that be ordained of God" and "Fear
God,Honour the King". But there is little reference to the need for
spiritual regeneration of the poor which later she was to stress so
much.

4. The pamphlets of 1795-98

The popular counter-revolutionary tracts of the later part of the
decade fall clearly into two categories. First there were those which
continue in the broad tradition of the 1792-93 tracts. The arguments,
techniques and styles established in those months of most intense
conflict were still often employed in a range of popular tracts, although inevitably the central concern became less the need to resist
internal subversion and more the necessity of pursuing the war until
Jacobinism was destroyed in France. Job Nott continued to address the
people of Birmingham. In More Advice from Job Nott (1795) he denounced
French and English Jacobins alike and urged his fellow artificers to
stand firm and do their patriotic duty. In 1798 he published a series of
horror stories about the activities of the French army in Germany in A
Front View of the Five Headed Monster. These overspilled into a second
pamphlet and chronicled both violence and slaughter and the multiple
rape of the pregnant and geriatric. Only their atheism, he argued,
allowed the French to act in this inhuman way and he warned that the
same things were "going on in Ireland, where French or Illuminati
principles prevail". To prevent "such horrid scenes" spreading to
England, he urges the men of Birmingham to join the British army, for
such mass enlistment will deter the French.

The second kind of counter-revolutionary pamphlet in the later part of the decade was Hannah More's _Cheap Repository Tracts_ (1795-98). These overwhelmingly dominated the second half of the decade in their frequency, regularity and circulation. They are quite different in character from the earlier pamphlets. The vast majority are moral and religious tracts with no explicit political content. Only a very few, like the _Loyal Sailor; or no Mutineering_ (1797), are directly political. Another small minority explicitly relate religious principles to current political and social problems. For example during the scarcity of 1795 More produced three apposite tracts. In July she published the ballad _Patient Joe, or the Newcastle Collier_ which urges the acceptance of hardship. In August she revived the characters of Jack Anvil and Tom Hod (from _Village Politics_) in a ballad _The Riot; or, Half a Loaf is better than no bread_, the distribution of which, she claimed, stopped a riot among Bath colliers. In September, in _The Way to Plenty_, she showed the poor how by wise housekeeping they could survive on very little, explaining how to prepare rice milk and vegetable stews. After pausing in 1796 to write a _Hymn of Praise for the Abundant Harvest_, she returned in her 1797 tract _The Cottage Cook_ to providing recipes for cheap but nourishing dishes. These tracts appear more like a pauper's cookery book than political propaganda, but they assume attitudes and values which are profoundly counter-revolution-ary. Scarcity and hardship provide an opportunity for the poor to show their strength of character by surviving adversity.

The religious arguments which in 1792-93 had provided only a final safetynet now dominate. The crucial political role which religion plays as an agent of social control is explored in More's _History of Mr Fantom_ (1797). This was a reaction to Paine's _Age of Reason_ (1795-96) and attacked the atheism of the _philosophes_ which she believed had inspired the French revolutionaries' political principles. Fantom, dominated by vanity and obsessed by speculative, universal benevolence, busies himself constructing huge impractical schemes to benefit the whole of mankind, but refuses to give any aid whatsoever, financial or practical, to help his needy neighbours. The humble, christian Mr Trueman, by contrast, devotes himself to good works - fighting fires, raising subscriptions, comforting the afflicted. More introduces a theological and philosophical argument into her simple and engaging tale. Fantom, in common with that strand of enlightenment thinking represented by Condorcet and Priestley, assumes perfectibility of man, while Trueman acknowledges the corruption of original sin. More insists that man is a fallen creature with a corrupt nature, that misery arises from man's sinfulness and that we should not "accuse governments of defects which belong to man" Moreover, she asserts, because man is corrupt he needs restraints, and here politics and religion come together for "the connection of jacobinism with impiety is inseparable" Both government and Christianity impose restraints and involve subordination, "in both cases the hatred arises from aversion to a superior". Men must accept the restraints both of religion and of government if they are to overcome their sinful nature and enjoy the rewards of heaven. Fantom's servant William, corrupted by the new philosophy, steals from his master, murders and ends in a condemned cell. William tells Fantom, "I should never have fallen into sin deserving of the gallows, if I had not overheard you say that there was no hereafter, no judgement, no future

65

reckoning". The idea that "death was only an eternal sleep, and hell and
judgement were but an invention of the priests to keep the poor in
order" led him directly to crime.

Atheism, Hannah More was quite clear, brought men to revolution and
anarchy. Religion ensured peace and civilisation. In The Sunday School
(?1797) her protagonist assures the farmer from whom she sought a
subscription that knowledge of the Bible is "the best security you can
have, both for the industry and obedience of your servants". Human
motives, like fear and prudence, are much weaker than religious ones
"which are backed with the sanctions of rewards and punishments, of
heaven and hell". But in both her serious and her popular writings More
insists that the better-off sections of society must genuinely share
that faith, not just cynically manipulate it. In Two Wealthy Farmers
(1796) Mr Bragwell adopts a position similar to that of Voltaire. He is,
he declares, "persuaded that religion is quite a proper thing for the
poor". He does not "think the multitude can ever be kept in order
without it" and adds, "we must have bits and bridles, and restraints for
the vulgar". Mr Worthy agrees, but argues that it must be taken further.
> The same restraints which are equally necessary for the
> people at large are equally necessary for men
> of every order, high and low, rich and poor,
> bond and free, learned and ignorant. If Jesus
> Christ died for no one particular rank, class
> or community, then there is no one rank, class
> or community exempt from the obedience to his
> laws enjoined by the Gospel.
However, while in the eternal court of heaven rich and poor would be
condemned equally for their atheism, on earth the poor are at greater
risk. Fantom's servant William makes this clear in his dying speech.
> A rich man, indeed, who throws off religion,
> may escape the gallows, because want does not
> drive him to commit those crimes which lead to
> it; but what shall restrain a needy man, who
> has been taught that there is no dreadful re-
> ckoning? Honesty is but a dream without the
> awful sanctions of heaven and hell. (9)

But the History of Mr Fantom is uncharacteristic of the Cheap
Repository Tracts as a whole in its concentration on the negative aspect
of propaganda - the discrediting and undermining of the actions and
ideas of the adversary. Generally the tracts aim to propagate the 'true
faith' in a positive way. Political and social systems depend for their
stability upon the widespread acceptance of a set of fundamental values.
These tracts seek to advance a value system which will eradicate the
shortcomings of eighteenth-century society while remaining wholly non-
revolutionary. Reform is limited to the individual heart; the established political system and social hierarchy are inviolable. The wealthy
and powerful must abandon dissolute ways, set a good example to the poor
and devote themselves to christian charity. The poor must be honest,
industrious and send their children to the Sunday Schools set up by
their social superiors. Life on earth is placed in an eschatological
dimension. No corrupt pleasure or rebellion in this brief life is worth
the risk of eternal punishment; every worldly suffering will be

compensated for by the joys of heaven.

5. Edmund Burke and the popular counter-revolutionary tracts

To what extent, then, do these popular tracts reflect the thinking of Edmund Burke, whose Reflections predate them all? In many ways his influence is limited. For much of the time the tracts address themselves to different topics to Burke; they avoid most of his philosophical and historical arguments and concern themselves with simple immediate issues he never discusses. Many of their detailed specific arguments owed less to Burke than to other established conservative writers. For example, many of the points made about equality are drawn from a sermon preached by Dr William Vincent, Headmaster of Westminster, in May 1792 and later reprinted under the title Short Hints upon Levelling (1792). The frequently drawn contrast between the happiness and peace of mind of rich and poor comes from Archdeacon Paley's Reasons for Contentment (1792), and one tract actually acknowledges its indebtedness to John Bowles's Protest against T.Paine's 'Rights of Man' (1792).(10) Moreover, much ammunition for the anti-Paine diatribes was drawn from the hostile and misleading Life of Paine (1791) written by George Chalmers under the pseudonym of Francis Oldys, supposedly a graduate of the University of Pennsylvania.

In general, Burke influenced not so much the direct arguments of the tracts as their general way of thinking. In a few pamphlets at the more 'intelligent' end of the popular market, Burke's flavour and tone dominate and his specific arguments can be traced. Thomas Bull's letter to his gentleman cousin presents Burkean ideas in far more direct a way than any of his coarser correspondance. It even cites Burke as an authority on the 1688 Revolution: "the Revolution of that time did not alter the hereditary government of this Kingdom, but left laws and doctrines as sacred as they were before. The Revolution in France hath abolished them all." The Englishman's Political Catechism (1792) also refers to the 1688 Revolution, arguing that the true rights of Enlish-men were won then by our ancestors and handed down to the present generation. John Bowles's three Dialogues (1792) are strongly Burkean; while omitting the religious arguments, they attempt to convey the concept of prescription in popular terms. A Caution against Levellers (1792) describes the nation in unmistakeably Burkean language: "it is a sort of partnership; and in England the partnership is at least of a thousand years standing".

But these four pamphlets are uncharacteristic. Generally Burke's influence is less direct. One of her biographers has described Hannah More's Village Politics as "Burke for Beginners" and indeed that tract may be seen as the most concentrated form of the more indirect in-fluence, though to a lesser degree Burke's attitudes are reflected in all the counter-revolutionary popular tracts.(11) Four themes pre-dominate. Firstly, and perhaps most significantly, the tracts adopt a wholly Burkean concept of Rights. The real rights of men are seen as the detailed privileges inherited from past generations within a specific society, not the speculative and universal rights of the philosophes and revolutionaries. The laws of England provide men with all the civil rights they require or to which they are entitled. An abstract concept

of equality is incompatible with civil society, equality obtains only
when men are savages back in the woods. Government should be based on
the actual experience of specific communities, not abstract theories of
Natural   Rights.   Ten Minutes Reflections on the late Events in France
(1792) ridicules a man who dismissed his old experienced tailor
complaining
>   you follow the old vulgar practice of taking
>   measure, which I am now too wise to submit to;
>   I am to send for the Professor of Anatomy, who
>   knows how a man is made by Nature, and he shall
>   cut my coat for me of that perfect pattern
>   which becomes it.

Secondly the tracts reflect Burke's prescriptive arguments, his
respect for tradition and established institutions. It is foolish to
tamper with a machine which runs efficiently or a government which
brings prosperity. Hannah More's Village Politics tells of how the
squire refused his wife's request to pull down his fine old castle and
replace it with a new French building. It was, he said, a castle built
on sound foundations by the wisdom of his ancestors, one which had
>   outstood the civil wars, and only underwent a
>   little needful repair at the Revolution, and
>   which all my neighbours come to take a pattern
>   by; - shall I pull it down, I say, only because
>   there may be a dark closet, or an awkward
>   passage or an inconvenient room or two in it?
In Principles of Order and Happiness (1792) a squire tells the parish
clerk that reform is possible, "but it would not be French, nor founded
on the Rights of Man: It must be the work of time and English good
sense". The complex balance between the three parts of the constitution,
which had been slowly established over the years, must not be disturbed.

Thirdly, the tracts reflect Burke's appreciation of the need for
sinful, corrupt man to be restrained by religious sanctions. Much of the
Reflections is devoted to an attack on the philosophes' atheism and this
is repeated in the tracts along with vivid illustrations of the violent
effects of the removal of such sanctions. In A Letter to a Member of the
National Assembly Burke suggested that the revolutionaries sought to
replace religious restraint and christian humility with "inordinate
vanity"; Rousseau, he alleged, was the "philosophic instructor in the
ethics of vanity". Apart from a few casual references in the 1792-93
tracts, it was not until More's History of Mr Fantom in 1797 that the
assault on vanity and speculative benevolence was carried into the
popular arena. Fourthly, some of the later tracts, though not those of
the Cheap Repository, reflect Burke's anti-Jacobin crusade and his
insistence that no false peace be made with a regicide nation. Jacobinism must be wholly destroyed and the French monarchy restored before
England can rest at peace.

Some aspects of the popular tracts clearly derive directly from
Burke. Many others are consonant with his viewpoint but explore issues
he ignored. A few are in direct conflict. Burke's impassioned defence of
Marie Antoinette, the French aristocracy and the ancien regime in Europe
have no echoes in the popular tracts. Louis XVI is admired and pitied,

but otherwise the tracts contrast the abuses of pre-revolutionary France to the benefits enjoyed in Britain. Secondly, Burke's defence of the aristocracy in Britain conflicts with the demand of John Bowdler in Reform or Ruin (1797), of Hannah More and of other tract writers that they reform their dissolute and immoral ways and set a better example. Thirdly, and most importantly, the popular tracts show a genuine concern and respect for the poor often lacking in Burke. Some specifically disclaim his reference to the "swinish multitude". The poor may be fallible and misled, but they are not contemptible. Occasionally, it is true, Burke had spoken of the poor with greater warmth but he never showed the real knowledge of and love for them evident in the Cheap Repository Tracts. The values of the rural world created in these stories came from More's own experience in the Mendips and her christian faith.

The counter-revolutionary popular propaganda of the 1790s not only draws upon the past but also points towards the future. Both the polemical, political and economic arguments of the 1792-93 pamphlets and the Christian vision of a caring rural community in the Cheap Repository Tracts were devoted to the idea of a united society. Any suggestion that different classes in the social hierarchy had conflicting economic interests was firmly denied. The existing social and economic structure provided plenty of opportunities for the industrious to improve themselves. The Cheap Repository Tracts, even more than the earlier pamphlets, stress that prosperity comes from a combination of effort and initiative with frugality and saving, and the attitudes of Samuel Smiles's Self Help (1859) are clearly prefigured in their pages. Hope of economic improvement on earth and of eternal reward in heaven provide the safety valves which reduce the pressure of nascent class conflict. The resulting vision of a whole community united in a common interest both rests upon an old rural tradition of social deference, stability and order, and looks forward, in a period of rapid industrialisation and urbanisation, to the future conservative notion of 'one nation'.

Notes

1. John Bull's Second Answer to his brother Thomas (1792) p.7; The Englishman and the Frenchman (1792) pp.7,4; One Pennyworth of Truth (1792) p.1.

2. J.Towers, Remarks on the Conduct, Principles and Publications of the Association at the Crown and Anchor... (1793) p.36.

3. The Life and Adventures of Job Nott... (1793), 11th ed.,1798, pp.32,6.

4. Liberty and Equality treated of in a short history addressed from a Poor Man to his Equals (1792) p.13.

5. A Plain and Ernest Address to Britons... (1792) p.4.

6. A few minutes advice to the People of Great Britain on Republics, (Bristol, 1792) p.9.

7. A few plain questions and a little honest advice to the Working People of Great Britain (1792) p.13.

8. A dialogue between Mr. T..., A Tradesman in the City and his Porter John W... (1792) p.8.

9. The final sentence does not appear in the 1798 and 1799 editions of the Cheap Repository Tracts. More added it later when including the story in her complete works.

10. A Plain and Ernest Address to Britons... (1792) p.1.

11. M.G.Jones, Hannah More, (Cambridge, 1952) p.134.

Fiction as Propaganda in the French Revolution

MALCOLM COOK

1. The Production of fiction and its audience

More full length novels were printed in France in 1789 than in any previous year. (1) This surprising fact might be explained in two ways - either readers were looking to the novel for an expression of political ideas; or they were looking to the novel to take them away from the realities of 1789. Certainly, the production of fiction dropped dramatically as the events moved towards the Republic of the Year II. Even the problem of dating works in years once the republican calendar was introduced cannot explain the dearth of fiction in 1793 and 1794. There was, of course, a paper shortage and, if we are to believe what one writer of fiction stated, the revolutionary wars had taken away many of the workers involved in the printing presses. (2)

While there was an understandable reduction in the number of full length novels, there were some notable exceptions. For example, La Nouvelle Héloïse by Jean-Jacques Rousseau, went through 14 separate editions from 1791-1800, not counting those in the complete works. Other forms of fictional writing were being produced - the theatres were producing plays of propaganda which were easily digested by the population. The written word was less accessible, although public readers in parks, clubs and cafés meant that many short fictional works had a 'readership' which full length novels did not.

The works of the major philosophes were not forgotten by the revolutionary public, (3) and, as Professor Darnton has pointed out, the anonymous and shocking libelles [lampoons], which were so popular in the last years of the Ancien Régime still also had an undoubted influence. (4) It is an impossible task to determine exactly what effect fictional works had on the propagation of ideas. But the fact that so many marginal works - that is works which avoided a straightforward presentation of ideas and preferred a fictional setting - were produced, must give us some idea of their popularity. One can look towards contemporary novels for some assessment of the standing of

fiction, but we will find inexplicable contradictions. (5) Novels are
not a reliable source of information about the status of fiction. One
can look towards archive material: what were colporteurs carrying in
their bags at the moment of arrest? But of course all we learn from
such inventories is what remained - perhaps other texts had already been
sold.

The Police Archives can give us some idea about the remainders, but
they present a particularly biased view: not all the records survived
the fire in the Prefecture during the Paris Commune in 1871. Those
archives which remain suggest that police activity concentrated
especially on works which were obviously licentious. Many arrests were
made, sometimes because booksellers were selling material which lacked
the name of printers or authors, sometimes because explicit engravings
allowed the non-reading 'policeman' to 'recognise' works contrary to
public morality. Some of the titles of works seized are indicative: Le
Bordel national (1790) [The National Brothel], Les Fureurs utérines de
Marie-Antoinette (1791) [Marie-Antoinette's uterine furies], Marie-
Antoinette dans l'embarras [Marie-Antoinette in a predicament]. The
archives betray an inconsistency which gives a clear idea of the
reality: many works were seized on the pretext that they appeared 'sans
nom d'auteur ni d'imprimeur' [without the name of the author or printer]
- but in fact it was the works 'garnis d'Estampes fort indécentes'
['illustrated with most indecent engravings'] which allowed easy
identification. Evidently, the liberty of the press achieved in 1789
was a relative concept which subjected a new class of booksellers to
constant harrassment by a police force which made arrests based on
facile judgements of texts.

2. Pornographic literature

In a sense we are introduced to one of the aspects of fiction as
propaganda. There was clearly a market for pornographic literature,
especially when the characters participating were aristocrats. The
reputation of the Queen was a constant impetus to writers attacking a
corrupt monarchy. The majority of these works, which include real
characters in fictional scenarios, function on a double register. They
are generally not sophisticated in literary terms, but their message is
perfectly adequate. The corrupt monarchy was seen to have given
political power to people who were, as an implied consequence, unworthy
of it. Public libraries give us an imprecise appreciation of the full
impact of many of these short pamphlets. Certainly, the written words
are clear enough for those who can read, but the engravings which both
attracted the reader and reinforced the message are often missing. La
Messaline française ou les nuits de la duchesse de Polignac [The French
Messalina or the nights of the Duchesse of Polignac] which appeared in
1790 is an account of a young man's arrival at court and his corruption
by the duchesse and her unnamed companion. The young man, having seen
the error of his ways, now confesses his nocturnal activities with the
duchesse. He writes, 'Oh I confess, my friend, that I have never seen a
woman with such energetic passion as the Duchesse de Polignac' (p. 59).
Finally the revolution arrived. The author realised that the duchesse
had participated in 'aristocratic' meetings but at the time he was

unaware of the nature of these meetings. Now his eyes are open, he spells out the clear message of the text:

> There, my friend, are the details you asked for:
> I am convinced that you will find them
> interesting; they allow you to see the conduct of
> those titled women whose opulence and arrogance
> crushed and treated with insolence modest
> bourgeois virtue. (p. 77)

There are, basically, two kinds of pornographic propaganda during the Revolution. The first, short pamphlets of perhaps 8-10 pages, were often dialogues involving known figures. The message was immediately apparent and accessible to a non-reading public through 'readers' in cafés and parks. The second category, the full length novel, is more rare, and often more subtle in its approach. It may have been too subtle to have had any serious impact. For example, Julie Philosophe [Julie the Philosopher] is a first-person memoir account of a girl's various love affairs. Some of her lovers are fictional characters, others are recognisable historical figures. The novel, in two volumes, appeared in 1791. Julie admires the revolution but rejects the suggestion that sexual licence has any relationship with civic virtue. Indeed, she is prepared to offer her body for the services of the state. Julie is a fervent supporter of Necker, Bailly and La Fayette. But this does not prevent an affair with Calonne which she justifies: 'I will encourage him to return to France and to use his enlightened views for the benefit of his fellow citizens'. (ii, p.28)

The novel seems an open apology for the middle classes, seen as the source of talent and virtue in the state:

> It is in the middle class, amongst the
> reasonably well-off that one finds the men who
> are most worthy because of their talents and
> their virtues. Far away from indigence to be
> able to cultivate their minds, but too far away
> from opulence and elevation for their hearts to
> be corrupted, to indulge in the vices which are a
> consequence, they live in tranquillity, without
> knowing the torments of ambition. (ii, p.70)

Julie Philosophe is a well-written novel offering a clear message in support of a moderate revolution. It fits the pattern of a number of novels of propaganda of the Revolution in that it produces an illusion of reality by a fusion of 'historical' characters and events with clearly fictional elements.

3. Fiction, politics and illusion.

Authors realised the political potential of fiction but varied the ingredients of their works in different ways. Many novels of 1789 - and indeed many novels of the post-1750 period - offered political statements which were almost lost in the mass of fictional elements and insipid moral statements. The novels could hardly be defined as political: but they do have a political content which offers a striking reminder of the reality beyond the fiction. Indeed, on occasions, the author is prepared to break the illusion of fiction to introduce a political bias. There was, of course, a long tradition of didactic fiction, of novels offering bland love-stories where general statements about the evils of luxury and vice and the virtues of poverty, chastity and charity proliferated. The political content of such novels is normally too general, too vague to be labelled as propaganda.

It would appear that one of the basic requirements of propaganda is clarity. There is of course a danger that excessive clarity might render the novel dogmatic and dull. The best of the revolutionary novelists avoid such a danger by proposing a blend of fiction and history, and by avoiding repeated overt statements. For example, Loaisel de Tréogate's novel <u>Ainsi finissent les grandes passions ou les dernières amours du Chevalier de ...</u> (Paris 1788) [<u>Thus finish great passions, or the last lives of the Chevalier de ...</u>] is not, by any extent, a political novel. It recounts the unhappy story of a Chevalier whose loved one is corrupted by society and becomes a frivolous coquette. The narrator interrupts his account with what is almost an aside:

> One thing, however, tempers the ideas which
> afflict me. It is the presence of our good King.
> When I see this young Prince who has the will and
> courage to be just, who distinguishes the truth
> behind passions, prejudice and his courtiers, and
> who thinks that glory belongs only to virtue;
> when I consider his scorn for luxury and
> ostentation, his simplicity, his joyous and
> satisfied air; it puts balm into my blood...
> (i, p.79)

It is possible, in general terms, to trace the progress of fictional propaganda by following the chronology of the revolution, at least as far as 1794/1795. During the days of the constitutional monarchy the taste was for short novels offering allegorical presentations of reality. These novels rarely posed any problems of interpretation and, almost invariably, proposed the same political viewpoint. The young King was innocent and good. Yet he inherited a corrupt court and was badly advised by wicked courtiers seeking self-advancement. In other words, the King needed assistance in his role - but he was not inherently bad. The allegorical forms of presentation can vary - but the Orient is favoured, even if the accuracy of the picture of the East is questionable.

The anonymous author of the <u>Royaume de Naudelit</u> [<u>The Kingdom of Naudelit</u>] (1789) explained the reasons for the subterfuge:

> So that it may interest a greater number of
> readers, force them even to agree about the
> necessity of the operations of the Estates-
> General, I have felt obliged to cover the gradual

progress of our Representatives with the veil of
allegory, so as not to offend the sensibility of
certain readers who might still be clinging to
the former systems.
(Preface, p.iii-iv)

The reasons given by the author are worth considering: allegory presents
a further interest over a straightforward account - it might be more
effective as a means of persuasion - it might shock those readers who
still favoured the Ancien Régime less by its removal of reality from
contemporary France.

Yet Le Royaume de Naudelit does not offer a historical account of
events - on the contrary, it proposes a prejudiced view of France with a
clear form of praise for the status quo. For example, we read:

The little shrub remains in its state of
mediocrity; it does not desire, like the oak
tree, to reach up towards the sky : the oak tree
does not attempt to devour the shrub; its
elevation is sufficient for it. (p. 51)

In other words, the class system is one which has a natural
justification - the poor and weak are happy to remain so, while the rich
and powerful are not seeking to devour them.

The use of allegorical stories as propaganda is, of course,
somewhat paradoxical. Propaganda of any sort seeks to propose a view
which, ideally, is to be accepted by readers. In order better to
educate, the writers of this form of fictional propaganda use subterfuge
and illusion at the expense of forthright statement. Bernardin de
Saint-Pierre was not alone in his defence of allegorical forms. In La
Chaumière Indienne [The Indian Cottage] (1791) he wrote:

We should not see the light of the sun if it did
not fix itself on certain bodies, or at least on
the clouds. It escapes outside our atmosphere
and dazzles us at its source. It is the same
for truth; we should not grasp it if it were not
attached to tangible events, or at least to
metaphors and comparisons which reflect it; it
needs a body to reflect it. (Foreword)

In other words, 'truth' is best expressed indirectly. Bernardin is
begging the question somewhat, in that he supposes the existence of
objective truth. It might have been more accurate to suggest that one's
particular prejudice is best expressed through a pleasing medium - the
indirect is more direct than the direct, paradoxical as this may appear.

The vast majority of these allegorical tales were published
anonymously. They tend to be favourable to the monarchy and this itself
is an indication of authorship. One such tale with the unlikely title,
Précis historique des causes principales qui ont amené la Révolution
présente dans l'Empire de la Cochinchine.   [Historical précis of the

principal causes which have brought about the present Revolution in the Cochin-China Empire] (1791) was, apparently, printed in Wimbledon! The imprint sounds improbable – yet it would not be surprising if a laboured critical account of the Revolution using barely disguised names was, indeed, written by an émigré living in England. Orléans ('le dégoûtant personnage') [the 'disgusting character'] takes the brunt of the attack while Louis and Marie-Antoinette are described sympathetically.

Fiction was certainly being used to further a political standpoint. But one wonders to what extent it was confirming people in their opinions rather than modifying their views. Many of the allegorical stories announce their intentions in the title: Le Règne du Prince Trop-Bon dans le royaume des fols [The reign of Prince Too-Good in the Kingdom of Fools] (1792) allows little room for surprise. It is, of course, a sympathetic account of Louis XVI and an attack on his ungrateful subjects. But would the story have made any new converts to the monarchist cause?

There were so many disguised versions of the Revolution using anagrams of names and invented oriental lands that contemporary readers looked for subterfuge even where there was none. So that the anonymous Anecdote historique traduite du turc [Historical anecdote translated from the Turkish] (1790) was assumed to be an allegorical presentation of the Revolution, but a perplexed critic admitted: 'We have understood nothing about this work except that there are some similarities with the present circumstances'. (6)

4. Social reportage.

Less popular, but not to be neglected, are a number of novels which claimed to reproduce contemporary reality in an 'objective' fashion. Again the overriding tendency was to produce accounts which were critical of the Revolution and which portrayed the masses as bloodthirsty ungrateful villains who hounded the poor aristocracy mercilessly and who professed no allegiance to the good King. The best known of these, and it is a novel which is readily available today, was Sénac de Meilhan's L'Emigré [The Emigré]. (7) Written in 1793, the first edition appeared in 1797. It was highly critical of the Revolution through the character of the Marquis de Saint Alban who wrote to his friend, the Président de Longueil:

> The majority of those who have been fortunate
> enough to escape with their lives from the
> monsters who govern France, find only misery
> in foreign lands. (p. 1570)

Novels which attacked the Revolution had to propose a dual defence of the King and of the nobility. The nobility was portrayed as benevolent and misunderstood. In Gorjy's Les Tablettes sentimentales du bon Pamphile [The Sentimental tablets of good Pamphile] (1791) the hero learns with anguish of the supposed death by drowning of the nobleman, the comte de Guérinval who was trying to escape from the revolutionary crowd. Pamphile discovers that the comte did not actually die – he meets him and listens to a pathetic defence: 'My poor vassals were always sure of assistance; I would have risked my own life to defend the life of the least of them. (p. 168) The villagers who rejected the comte were led astray by brigands who frightened them into expelling the nobleman. Now, thanks to Pamphile and the village priest, the villagers see the error of their ways and peace returns to the village.

This novel, and a similar one, Liomin's La Bergère d'Aranville [The Shepherdess of Aranville] (1792), propose critical views of the Revolution by showing virtuous noblemen confronted by revolutionary brigands. The reality described in these novels is not a precise historical one. The characters are fictional and the events are imagined. There are no references to specific events yet the verisimilitude is an essential factor of the propaganda. In other words, if the reality is rejected, the political message is lost.

5. The pastoral tale.

It would appear, from what has been said so far, that fictional propaganda was a one-way affair. This is true up to a point. The point in question is the arrival of the Republic in 1792. During Year II fictional propaganda took a dramatic turn. There was a sudden increase in fictional works of an extremely simple kind proposing a straightforward message of republican virtue. The medium favoured was the pastoral tale.

Florian had provided the foundations for this kind of literature by renewing a literary tradition. Florian's shepherds and shepherdesses had met with great favour from the contemporary readership. He was not unaware of the value of the pastoral for propaganda purposes. In his Essai sur la pastorale [Essay on the Pastoral] (1788) which prefaced his novel, Estelle, he wrote: 'As soon as one announces a work in which the heroes are shepherds, it seems that the very mention of shepherds makes one want to sleep' (p.3). But he maintained that Pastorals could be given a particular meaning. They could teach 'des leçons d'une morale pure et douce' ['sweet; pure, moral lessons'] (p.39). Moreover they could serve to improve the lot of the peasant: 'Such books would, I believe, be neither boring nor futile; and the poor in the villages would soon notice if their lord was reading them' (p. 39).

Of course, Florian was exceptional. His works were seen as examples of pastoral literature which were perfectly suited to the sensibilities of the Republic. He was proposing in fiction what Robespierre was proposing in his reports and speeches: a glorification of the natural state which the festivals and ceremonies of Year II seemed to wish to embody. (8) Few writers managed to match Florian's standards - but many tried. The Republic used the pastoral for propaganda in the same way that the Monarchy used the Orient. Each régime favoured a particular allegory.

Pierre Blanchard's Félix et Pauline (1793-4) is a good example of this new form of republican propaganda. It is an unhappy love story designed to move the reader into acceptance of simple rustic virtues.

We read in the Foreword: '... I have tried to inspire the love of
simplicity and nature : simplicity is the first virtue of the
Republican, and nature presents happiness to the free man'. The plot of
the novel is excessively simple. Two men decide to marry their children
to each other. A rich suitor presents himself and the girl's father
succumbs to the temptation. Pauline the girl, is horrified but agrees
to obey her father (filial duty is a republican virtue). Félix hears of
the planned marriage and kills himself. Pauline, languishes, her
proposed marriage is called off, and the couple will eventually find
union in heaven. Virtue is not rewarded, but the message of the novel
is clear. Sordid hopes of financial gain will bring misery. Happiness
is to be found in simplicity and virtue. Republican propaganda hoped to
educate through the exaggerated sensibility of its pastoral heroes.

6. Fiction and propaganda: the English dimension.

It is clear that writers felt that fiction could have a political
significance and a propaganda value which a straightforward treatise or
account might not have. The audience was, presumably, quite different.
How effective the propaganda was is impossible to gauge. One must have
some reservations since it would appear that readers tend to read what
they like to hear. The problem with propaganda is either that it is too
obvious and therefore not interesting, or too complex and therefore not
obvious! It should not be forgotten that many writers were aiming
specifically at children. Here simplicity was an essential requirement,
as too was brevity and clarity.

One finds propaganda in every kind of novel. The licentious novel,
comic and suggestive, was able to offer a coherent political statement.
Louvet de Couvray's Les Amours du Chevalier de Faublas [The Loves of
the Chevalier de Faublas] (1787-90) which is essentially a comic novel
of sexual antics written by a man who was later to become a member of
the Convention and an enemy of Robespierre, offered a clear republican
statement before the fall of the Bastille. It must be assumed that he
saw the novel form as a means of reaching an audience which conventional
political tracts would not. This would seem to be the essential quality
of fictional progaganda.

The value of fictional propaganda did not go unnoticed across the
Channel. There is something paradoxical about the nature of this
fiction. When written in France for French readers, fiction had to
produce an illusion of reality which could be at odds with the personal
experience of the reader : it had to produce a convincing picture of
reality which might not be not that of the reader. The reader in France
knew his reality at first hand. There was no point in showing the
prevalence of brigands and massacres if such things were not within the
reader's sphere of knowledge. In other words, French writers, producing
works for the French audience had a double difficulty. They had to
produce an illusion of reality which could be seen as actually real.
Writers of propaganda in England who were producing works for the
English audience had no such difficulty. Those who were critical of the
Revolution produced works showing the horrors of France since 1789.
Those who were in favour would concentrate on the benefits of the

BRF-F

Revolution. In both cases the effectiveness of the propaganda hinged on the credibility of the reality described.

We are faced with the paradox that propaganda is more likely to be effective from a distance. It was not the realism of the novels which had the greatest impact but the biased nature of the reality portrayed. There was a further problem of course - writers describe what they want to describe and select that reality which best suits their purpose. The English reader would have had great difficulty in deciding what was real and what was fictional if he had read nothing but novels! Furthermore, how did he decide what were 'novels' and what were 'authentic' accounts - since no novels would accept fictional status?

For example, Helen Maria Williams, in her Letters written in France in the summer 1790 to a friend in England: containing several anecdotes relative to the French Revolution, which, by 1796, had seen five editions and had been translated into French is, apparently, not a novel. But it could be! The distinction between fiction and reality is minimal when the reality described defines the moral of the work. The first letter describes the Fête de la Fédération, held in July 1790 to celebrate the first anniversary of the fall of the Bastille:

> The weather proved very unfavourable during
> the morning of the Federation; but the minds
> of the people were too much elevated by ideas
> of moral good to attend to the physical evils
> of the day. (p. 14)

How does the author know what was in the minds of the participants? And why do contemporary engravings not show the rain teeming down and the participants dripping with water? And where were the puddles and the mud on the Champ-de-Mars which had been especially prepared for the celebration. Clearly, propaganda bears only an oblique relationship to truth. Indeed, the very nature of truth is determined by one's beliefs.

In 1791 a novel appeared anonymously entitled, Lindor and Adelaide, a moral tale in which are exhibited the effects of the late French Revolution on the peasantry of France. It was printed in London and signed by "The author of Observations on Dr. Price's Revolution Sermon". A French translation appeared in Paris the following year. The author, it appears, was Goodricke, of whom next to nothing is known. Certainly he wrote no other novels. The title of the novel gives nothing away, but the reader is not long left in doubt about the nature of the work: we are to read the story of two young people in a village near Grenoble, 'whose short and unhappy history is the subject of the following relation, and whose singular fate it was to derive all their misery from the political situation of their country...'. (p. 1-2)

The introduction leaves little doubt about the nature of the novel. Lindor and Adelaide, virtuous lovers, have been brought up in the same village near Grenoble. The village was a haven of peace and restfulness; it was a perfect microcosm of society with a benevolent lord of the manor, the Marquis d'Antin, farmers and peasants. We read:

> The farmer lived in ease and affluence while
> the lord maintained and shared his dignity
> and his splendour with those who supported
> both. The peasant paid the easy and honourable
> tribute of respect with willingness, nay with
> zeal. While he received in return the solid
> advantages of security and peace. (p. 4)

We learn that the Marquis d'Antin had fought during the American War of
Independence – that he had been wounded in battle but had returned to
the village. Now he and his wife have been called to Versailles to
assist the King.

It appears that the Marquis is now finding life financially
difficult. He has been obliged to sell the mansion next to his to the
Levilles, a family of bankers from Paris. The two worlds come face to
face on the road. The Marquis, on the way to Versailles, passes the
Levilles arriving to take up residence:

> In his way he met the gaudy carriage of the
> Levilles on the road; they passed by him
> with swelling hearts but their mean deportment,
> as they approached, sunk before the consciousness
> of real nobility and superior worth. (p. 13–14)

The scene is set for a confrontation of different life-styles and
opposing values. We now meet the two lovers: Adelaide has been brought
up by Maricour, an old woman aged over 80, and by the village priest
(who is 80 in the English version but only 70 in the French). Maricour,
the guardian of the d'Antin's house, is very much a supporter of the
nobility. Lindor is the son of a merchant in Marseilles; he has been
raised by his aunt in the village.

Adelaide's guardian, the priest, warns her about her affection for
Lindor – he has, apparently, 'imbibed' some dangerous principles. He
is, at heart, a good soul: 'Cheerful and gay, he delighted in the
labours of the field.' (p. 85) He rejects offers of rapid social
advancement in Marseilles. His marriage to Adelaide is his only
ambition. But Lindor supports the Revolution – and this is an obstacle
in the path of true love. The priest intervenes and gives him a long
sermon. Lindor asks: 'Is it not unjust that one man should be absolute
master of so many, seeing they are all equal by birth?' (p. 90) The
priest reasons with Lindor, pointing out the need for governments – 'the
whole is too unwieldy to govern itself' (p. 106) – and even justifying
despotism – India, constantly under foreign attack, needs a despot for
quick action:

> Governments, therefore, must suit themselves
> to the wants of the governed; it is they who
> are to be pleased, not a few speculative
> philosophers in Geneva. (p. 109)

The priest maintains that France needs a strong and powerful
monarchy to protect it from Spain and Germany. It needs a nobility too,

both in order to provide a barrier between the King and his subjects and to provide a means of defence. It is suggested that exempting the nobility from taxation is cheaper than hiring mercenaries to protect the state.

The priest's moralising has a demoralising effect on Lindor. He sleeps badly and dreams that the King is attacked and a dagger is held to his throat.

Eventually, Lindor comes face to face with the Levilles. Following his long discussion with the priest, Lindor is now more sceptical about the values of the Revolution. Mme Leville tries to overcome his doubt: 'we are all equal you see', she states, to which Lindor replies:

> No, I don't see that. I have no sumptuous house,
> keep no magnificent table, drink no wine, and
> can scarcely afford to buy myself a pitiful
> dinner; while you have horses and houses, and
> even your equals, men, at your command. (p. 240)

Mme Leville fails to convince Lindor. Next morning a village assembly takes place. There is a suggestion that the d'Antin's castle should now be forfeited as they have emigrated to England. Lindor speaks against the proposal, is beaten up and dies from his wounds.

Meanwhile, an English friend of the d'Antins has arrived in the village to report on the state of the castle. He is shown round by Maricour who proudly reveals the charity book kept by the Marquis. It contains a list of all the villagers, their names and employment, 'and such small sums set against their names as were necessary for their occasional relief'. (p. 305). The Englishman mocks the French: 'Inestimable novelty! Liberty is to be procured by the abolition of law, and society is to be improved by the dissolution of order.' (p. 312)

Maricour and the Englishman then return to Maricour's cottage – to find Lindor dead and Adelaide suffering agonies of remorse. She develops a fever, dies of a broken heart, and is buried alongside Lindor. That night the castle is set on fire by the revolutionary mob. The Englishman is asked to return to England and tell Englishmen what he has seen: that they might beware of imitating the French and value better the nature of their own liberty.

<u>Lindor and Adelaide</u> is, obviously, a highly critical account of the Revolution. It manages to combine a specific view of a revolutionary reality with the 'sensibilité' of the moral novel. Its political significance is evident – clearly an English readership is intended to be shocked and disgusted by the events over the Channel. Indeed, by the end of the novel, we are presented with a first-person witness who is English and who returns to England for the very purpose of 'educating' his compatriots. But the novel also appeared in French – are we to assume that the French enjoyed English people writing about them? Is the novel intended for the pleasure of <u>émigrés</u>? Or are French people being asked to compare their own reality with that described in the novel?

It is hard to imagine the convinced revolutionary having the
patience to finish the novel; its biased account is provocative. But it
is possibly the case that propaganda of this kind would have a
confirmative purpose. In other words, people like reading what they
like to hear and what they themselves believe.

Goodricke's novel is a striking one; it is well-written in elegant
prose; it contains a cross-section of society - and it confronts the old
and the new elite in a deliberate manner. But its message is rather
obvious - and this appears to be the general case with fictional
propaganda.

Not all English novels were critical of the Revolution. Indeed,
the reality described in Charlotte Smith's novel Desmond (1792) which
appeared in French in 1793, is quite different from that of Goodricke.
Desmond goes out of his way to provide a corrective : the stories of
bloodthirsty brigands and anarchy which were spread by émigrés in
England were untrue. Helen Williams had said much the same thing in her
Letters written in France in the Summer of 1790:
> One cause of the general dislike in which the
> French Revolution is held in this country,
> is the exaggerated stories which are carefully
> circulated by such of the aristocrats as have
> taken refuge in England. (p. 222)

7. Conclusion.

It is not easy to assess the value of fictional propaganda, but it
is important to remember that it was used both in favour of the Revolution and against it. Historical events modify the reading process and
impose external constraints on the writer. Even when he tries to distance himself from the reality around him, the reader may well see the
act of separation as a political act and interpret the work accordingly.

The very nature of a fictional reality is that it invites
comparison with the reader's own reality. When writers claim they are
giving a picture of the French Revolution they are really doing little
more than emphasizing the particular refined nature of their chosen
reality. One cannot accept that the reality described is in any sense
more 'real' simply because it borrows familiar events or even
recognisable characters. But the significance, in terms of propaganda,
will depend to a great extent on the bias of the fictional
representation. In the final event, the effectiveness of the propaganda
will depend on the reader. Propaganda may encourage him to question
some of his beliefs or it may confirm him in his opinions - writers of
propaganda during the Revolutionary period saw the value of fiction not
as a means of conviction but as a manner in which to get ideas read.
There remains a paradox: fictional propaganda aims to convince those
people for whom it is written, but it is more effective at a distance.
The reader who appreciates the difference between his reality and the
reality of the novel will turn away from the realistic novels : this
perhaps explains the popularity of different kinds of allegorical
presentation. The veil of fiction was more effective than the
straightforward account. Distance was more effective than proximity.

Notes

1. For fuller details, see R. Frautschi, A. Martin & V. Mylne, Bibliographie du genre romanesque français, London & Paris, 1977. There were 101 new novels which appeared in French, of which 58 were composed in French and 43 were translations. This figure does not include marginal works or re-editions. The production of novels drops progressively until 1794, when only 16 novels appeared, 14 French and 2 translations. By 1799, 174 novels were appearing, 123 of which were French, and 51 translations.

2. A.T. de Rochefort, in his novel Adraste et Nancy V.Y. Anecdote américaine, Saint-Maixent, Year II noted (p. 190): 'The difficulty that printers in the departments experience in getting workers has delayed publication until now'.

3. See, for example, A. Soboul, 'L'audience des Lumières sous la Révolution', in Utopies et institutions au XVIIIe. siècle, Paris, 1963, pp. 289-303. R. Galliani has studied the influence of the philosophes on the writers of revolutionary pamphlets. See his 'Voltaire cité dans les brochures de 1789', Studies on Voltaire and the 18th century, 132, 1975, pp. 17-54; 'La présence de Voltaire dans les brochures de 1790', Ibid., 169, 1977, pp. 69-114; and 'Voltaire et les autres philosophes dans la Révolution: les brochures de 1791, 1792, 1793', Ibid., 174, 1978, pp. 69-112.

4. R. Darnton, 'The High Enlightenment and the low life of literature in prerevolutionary France', Past and Present, 51, 1971, pp. 81-115.

5. Jean Devaines, Lettres de la Comtesse de ** au Chevalier de **, n.p.n.d. (1789?). The Comtesse complains that she can find (p. 7): 'Not a play for the theatre, not a single novel, only the many pamphlets of the day'. However, in the Lettres d'un Indien à Paris by L.A. Caraccioli, Amsterdam & Paris, 1789, we read (i, p. 300): 'You are quite wrong to send me to look at the brochures of the day ... only so-called English novels are being published, and it is certainly not in them that one must look for something agreeable and pleasing to read'.

6. Anon., Annonces de bibliographie moderne, Paris, 1790, i, p. 249-50.

7. It is available in Romanciers du XVIIIe. siècle, ed. Etiemble, Paris, 1965, ii, pp. 1541-1912.

8. See, by way of example, the Rapport présenté au nom du comité de salut public, 18 floréal an II, sur les rapports des idées religieuses et morales avec les principes républicains et sur les fêtes nationales. In Robespierre, Discours et rapports à la Convention, Paris, 1965, pp. 245-86. Notably (p. 249): 'Yes, this delicious land which we inhabit, and which nature caresses with predilection, is made to be the domain of liberty and happiness'.

BIBLIOGRAPHICAL NOTES

General and Introductory

There is a large but rather dispersed and allusive literature on relations between England and France in the eighteenth century. For an excellent summary see J.Bromley, 'Britain and Europe in the eighteenth century', History, 1981. D.Jarrett, The Begetters of Revolution: England's involvement with France 1759-89 (London, 1973), and F.Acomb, Anglophobia in France 1763-89: an essay in the history of constitutionalism and nationalism (Durham, North Carolina, 1950) both offer interesting information and insights. A general overview of the conflict between the two countries is provided in the section by J.Bromley and J.Meyer, entitled 'The Second Hundred Years War 1689-1815' of D.Johnson, F.Bedaride, F.Creuzot eds., Britain and France: ten centuries (London, 1980).

No satisfactory account exists of the Anglo-French conflict in the 1790s. The course of the struggle can best be followed perhaps, on the French side, in general histories of the Revolution: G.Lefebvre, The French Revolution 2 vols (London, 1962, 1967) and A.Soboul, The French Revolution 1787-99 2 vols (London, 1974) and probably the most helpful in this respect. On the English side, until the forthcoming appearance of the second volume of John Ehrman's The Younger Pitt, the basic account from the government's viewpoint remains J.H.Rose, William Pitt and the Great War (London, 1911). A broad survey of foreign policy is contained in J.M.Sherwig, Guineas and gunpowder: British foreign aid in the wars with France 1793-1815 (Cambridge, Mass., 1969), and a number of particularly good monographs on different aspects of the struggle. Some of the latter are mentioned below, but see too P.Mackesy, Statesmen at war: the strategy of overthrow 1798-99 (London, 1974).

For the impact of the Revolution and war on English and French society, see the refreshing introduction to the topic by G.Best, War and society in Revolutionary Europe 1770-1870 (Leicester, 1982). J.Deschamps, Entre la guerre et la paix: les Iles Britanniques et la Révolution Française 1789-1803 (Brussels, 1949) is out of date and rather over-literary in its approach, but contains a great deal of valuable material. On the French side, general histories of the Revolution should be consulted. Note in addition pathbreaking recent work on the social history of warfare in Revolutionary France, particularly S.F.Scott, The response of the royal line army to the French Revolution (Oxford, 1978) and J.P.Bertaud, La Révolution armée (Paris, 1979).

On the English side, the bracing synthesis of C.Emsley, British society and the French wars 1789-1815 (London, 1979) should be

consulted. This work also contains a useful introduction to the debate
on the democratic movement in England in the 1790s, which has become
something of an industry in recent years. The best introductions to
recent research are still probably G.A.Williams, Artisans and
sans-culottes: popular movements in France and England during the French
Revolution (London, 1968) and the still unsurpassed survey in
E.P.Thompson, The making of the English working class (London, 1963 and
Penguin edition 1968). Further new information on the democratic
movement in the provinces in particular may be found in A.Goodwin, The
Friends of Liberty: the English democratic movement in the age of the
French Revolution (London, 1979).

British policy in the war against Revolutionary France

The most recent broad survey of the Revolutionary and Napoleonic
wars from the British point of view is J.M.Sherwig, Guineas and
gunpowder: British foreign aid in the wars with France 1793-1815
(Cambridge, Mass., 1969), though the Cambridge History of British
Foreign Policy 1783-1919 vol 1 A.W.Ward and G.P.Gooch eds. (Cambridge,
1919) is still useful. M.Duffy's thesis 'British war policy: the
Austrian alliance 1793-1801' (DPhil, Oxford, 1971) contains a great deal
that is directly relevant. See the same author's '"A particular
service": the British government and the Dunkirk expedition of 1793',
English Historical Review, 1976.The government's justification for its
policies can be followed in R.Coupland ed., War Speeches of William Pitt
(London, 1915). For Wickham's activities in fostering counter-
revolution, see W.R.Fryer, Republic or restoration in France ?
(Manchester, 1965) and H.Mitchell, The underground war against
Revolutionary France (Oxford, 1965). See too M.Hutt, 'Spies in
France,1793-1808', History Today, 1962. The evolution of British plans
for the resettlement of Europe can be followed in J.M.Sherwig, 'Lord
Grenville's plan for a concert of Europe 1797-99', Journal of Modern
History, 1962; in J.H.Rose, Napoleonic Studies (London, 1906); and
C.K.Webster, The foreign policy of Castlereagh (London, 1947).
A.D.Harvey, 'European attitudes to Britain during the French
Revolutionary and Napoleonic era', History, 1978 shows some of the
European response.

The Anglo-French conflict in the Caribbean in the 1790's

The standard work on the British West Indies in this period is
L.J.Ragatz, The fall of the planter class in the British Caribbean

1763-1833, (Washington, D.C., 1928), whose thesis of West Indian decline is challenged by Seymour Drescher, Econocide: British slavery in the era of abolition (Pittsburgh, 1977). J.R.Jones, Britain and the world 1649-1815 (London, 1980) is a stimulating and original overview of commercial, military and foreign policy. J.Walvin ed., Slavery and British society 1776-1846 (London, 1982) examines the impact of the slavery question on British politics and opinion. The best work on the Saint Domingue revolution remains C.L.R.James, The Black Jacobins 3rd edition (London, 1980). T.Ott, The Haitian Revolution (Knoxville, 1976) provides an alternative approach. On French West Indian society, the numerous works of G.Debien are indispensable. F.Girod, La Vie quotidienne de la société créole (Paris, 1972) is a convenient introduction. The classic study of the West Indian campaigns of the 1790s is J.W.Fortescue, History of the British Army vol 4 (London, 1906) which offers an eloquent though biased account. On the black regiments, see R.N.Buckley, Slaves in red coats the British West India regiments 1795-1815 (New Haven, 1979). A reassessment of all aspects of the Saint Domingue venture is attempted in D.Geggus, Slavery, war and revolution: the British occupation of Saint Domingue 1793-8 (Oxford, 1982) which should be supplemented by the same author's 'The cost of Pitt's Caribbean campaigns 1793-8', Historical Journal, forthcoming 1983. For the French colonies during the Revolution, see J.Saintoyant, La colonisation française pendant la Révolution 1789-99 (Paris, 1930) and H.Lemery, La Révolution française à la Martinique (Paris, 1936). On colonial politics see G.Debien, Les colons de Saint-Domingue et la Révolution: essai sur le Club Massiac (Paris, 1953).

French subversion in Britain in the French Revolution

The topic of French revolutionary subversion abroad is still a relatively new one. The most recent material on the topic will be found in Marianne Elliott, Partners in Revolution: the United Irishmen and France (London, 1982). The same author's articles should also be consulted: 'The Despard conspiracy reconsidered', Past and Present, 1977; 'The origins and transformation of early Irish republicanism', International Review of Social History, 1978; and 'Irish republicanism in England: the first phase', in Golden era and penal age: essays in Irish history, T.Bartlett and D.Hayton eds., (Belfast, 1979). There is a wealth of original documentation derived from French archives in E.Desbrière, Projets et tentatives de debarquement aux Îles Britanniques 4 vols (Paris, 1900-2) and L.D.Woodward, 'Les projets de descente en Irelande et les refugiés irlandais et anglais en France sous la Convention', Annales Historiques de la Révolution Française, 1931.

For Ireland and the French Revolution, the best short survey is still T.Pakenham, The Year of Liberty (London, 1966), though there are good accounts also in J.C.Beckett, The making of modern Ireland (London, 1966) and R.Kee, The Green Flag: a history of Irish nationalism (London, 1972).

For the democratic movement in England in the 1790s see the works referred to above. The topic is closely tied up with the history of the British secret services. For an excellent account of the working of these at the time, see J.A.Hone, <u>For the cause of truth: radicalism in London 1796-1821</u> (Oxford, 1982). This theme is also pursued in the works of Clive Emsley: besides this general survey on Britain and the French wars cited above, see also his 'The Home Office and its sources of information and investigation 1791-1801', <u>English Historical Review,</u> 1979 and, 'An aspect of Pitt's "Terror": prosecutions for sedition during the 1790s', <u>Social History</u>, 1981. M.I.Thomis and P.Holt, <u>Threats of revolution in Britain 1789-1848</u> (London, 1977) should also be consulted — though with caution, for its conclusions on the 1790s at least are rather premature. Its sections on Scotland are particularly valuable, however, since for this topic we are still dependent on H.W.Meikle, <u>Scotland and the French Revolution</u> (Glasgow, 1912). Other older works also worth consulting include, on the Nore and Spithead naval mutinies, C.Gill, <u>The naval mutinies of 1797</u> (Manchester, 1913); D.Bonner-Smith, 'The naval mutinies of 1797', <u>Mariners Mirror</u>, 1935; and B.Dobree and G.E.Manwaring, <u>The Floating Republic</u> 3rd edition (London, 1937)

On the workings of British intelligence abroad see, (besides the works of Fryer and Mitchell cited above) two articles by A.Cobban: 'British secret service in France 1784-92', <u>English Historical Review,</u> 1954; and 'The beginning of the Channel Isles correspondence' <u>ibid,</u> 1962. For French undercover activities in countries other than Britain, there are gleanings to be had in S.S.Biro, <u>The German policy of Revolutionary France</u> 2 vols (Cambridge, Mass., 1957); A.Méautis, <u>Le Club Helvétique de Paris</u> (1790-1) et la diffusion des idées révolutionnaires en Suisse (Neuchatel, 1969); T.C.W.Blanning, <u>Reform and revolution in Mainz</u> (Cambridge, 1974); and S.Schama, <u>Patriots and liberators: revolution in the Netherlands 1780-1813</u> (London, 1977).

British Counter-revolutionary Popular Propaganda in the 1790's

While a number of editions of Burke's <u>Reflections on the Revolution in France</u> are available, including a Penguin one (1969), very few of the popular tracts have been reprinted since the 1790s. Hannah More's <u>Village Politics</u> and those of the Cheap Repository Tracts she wrote herself appear in her <u>Works</u> which ran into many editions in the nineteenth century. Alfred Cobban, <u>The Debate on the French Revolution 1789-1800</u> 2nd edition (London, 1960) includes some brief extracts from the Association papers and from Hannah More.

The popular tracts are directly discussed in three works. A.D.Harvey, <u>Britain in the early nineteenth century</u> (London, 1978) discusses both the serious and popular pamphlets and the caricature prints. R.K.Webb,The British working class reader 1790-1848 (London, 1955; reprinted 1971) examines the tracts in the context of working class literacy and culture. M.G.Jones, Hannah More (Cambridge, 1952), the most intelligent of the biographies, devotes a chapter to the 'Tracts' and one to 'The Schools'.

The radical movement to which these tracts were a response is examined in the works cited above, E.P.Thompson, The making of the English working class and A.Goodwin, The Friends of Liberty. The political climate of late 1792 and establishment fears are discussed in C.Emsley, 'The London "Insurrection" of December 1792: fact, fiction or fantasy ?', The Journal of British Studies, 1978 and in E.C.Black, The Association: British extra-parliamentary political organisation 1769-1793 (Cambridge, Mass., 1963).

Austin Mitchell, 'The Association Movement of 1792-93', Historical Journal, 1961 discusses the growth and strength of the movement, and D.E.Grinter, 'The Loyalist Association movement of 1792-93 and British public opinion' Historical Journal, 1966 stresses the variety of opinion within it. The cartoons and prints are authoritatively discussed in M.D.George, English political caricature: a study of opinion and propaganda 2 vols (Oxford, 1959). A.Aspinall, Politics and the press c. 1780-1850 (London, 1949) discusses government sponsorship of pamphlets as well as providing a general discussion of the role of newspapers.

More generally, H.T.Dickinson, Liberty and property: political ideology in eighteenth century Britain (London, 1977) provides a useful discussion of conservative ideology on an intellectual level, and John Stevenson, 'Social control and the prevention of riots in England, 1789-1829' in A.P.Donajgrodzki ed., Social control in nineteenth century Britain (London, 1977) examines wider methods of social control. Finally, studies of two ways in which religion was used to support radical movements, rather than conservative ones, are provided in J.E.Cookson, The Friends of Peace: anti-war liberalism in England 1793-1815 (Cambridge, 1982) especially chapter 5 'The Impact of Loyalism', a discussion of the anti-war Dissenters, and J.F.C.Harrison, The Second Coming: popular millenarianism 1780-1850 (London, 1979) chapter 4, an examination of the political implications of popular prophecy in 1794-95.

Fiction as propaganda in the French Revolution

There are few works which deal specifically with French prose fiction during the Revolution. Accurate statistical evidence can be found in R.Frantschi, A.Martin, V.Mylne eds., Bibliographie du genre romanesque français, (London and Paris, 1977). Useful background reading on the book trade in the 1780s is provided by R.Darnton's articles:

"Reading writing and publishing in eighteenth century France: a case study in the sociology of literature', Daedalus, 1971; and 'Le livre français à la fin de l'Ancien Régime', Annales.E.S.C., 1973. On the prevalence of lampoons, see the same author's 'The High Enlightenment and the low life of literature in prerevolutionary France', Past and Present, 1971. There are two recent studies of prose fiction during the Revolution: A.Martin, 'Le roman en France sous la Révolution, thèses et tendances', Studi francesi, 1972; and M.Cook, 'Politics in the fiction of the French Revolution 1789-94', Studies on Voltaire and the Eighteenth Century, 1982. A sample of revolutionary short stories can be found in M.Cook ed., Contes révolutionnaires, Exeter, Textes littéraires, 1982. For useful comparative reading on propaganda in other media, see J.Leith, The idea of art as propaganda in France 1750-99: a study in the history of ideas (Toronto, 1965); and M.Carlson, The theatre of the French Revolution (Cornell, 1966). See too A.Patrick, 'Paper, posters and people: official communication in France 1789-94', Historical Studies, 1978; and L.A.Hunt, 'Print and propaganda in the French Revolution', History Today, 1980.

BIOGRAPHICAL NOTES

Michael Duffy is lecturer in history at the University of Exeter. Among his publications are The Military Revolution and the state, 1500-1800, Exeter Studies in History 1, Exeter, 1980; and The Englishman and the Foreigner, forthcoming. He is preparing a book on the war against Revolutionary France.

David Geggus is the author of Slavery, war and revolution: the British occupation of Saint Domingue, Oxford, 1982, and of over twenty articles published in scholarly journals. He has recently been appointed Assistant Professor in the History Department, University of Florida, Gainesville.

Colin Jones is lecturer in history at the University of Exeter. He is the author of Charity and 'bienfaisance': the treatment of the poor in the Montpellier region, 1740-1815, Cambridge, 1982; editor of Contre Retz: sept pamphlets du temps de la Fronde, Exeter, Textes littéraires, 1982; and has published articles on a variety of topics in French social history from the early seventeenth to the early nineteenth century.

Malcolm Cook is a lecturer in the French Department at the University of Exeter. He was co-author of the 18th century section of The Year's Work in Modern Language Studies, 1979-1982, and the author of Politics in the Fiction of the French Revolution, 1789-1794, Studies on Voltaire and the Eighteenth Century, 201, pp. 233-340, and editor of a collection of short stories of the revolutionary period, Contes révolutionnaires, University of Exeter, Textes littéraires, XLV, xxiii + 71p. He has also written articles on Laclos and is currently preparing a book on fiction as propaganda.

Robert Hole is a lecturer at Rolle College, Exmouth. His M.A. dissertation was on 'Joseph Priestley and the Enlightenment' and he is currently researching on the role of religion on British political thought in the late eighteenth century.

Dr Marianne Elliott is author of Partners in Revolution : the United Irishmen and France (Yale University Press, 1982) and a number of articles on France and the British Isles during this period. She teaches for the Open University and has taught for the University of Warwick and University College of Swansea.